End Games in Chess

The Essential Techniques for Winning

by Theo Schuster

LUTTERWORTH PRESS · GUILDFORD AND LONDON

Translated by Joachim Liebschner
Cover design by Hans-Ulrich Eichler
from a design by Uwe Höch

ISBN 0 7188 2326 5

Printed in Great Britain by
William Clowes & Sons Limited
London, Beccles and Colchester

Contents

3

Foreword

Maybe you feel about the end game as I did some time ago? A beginner considers it a necessary evil. One aims at having very concise end game situations, perhaps Queen v. Rook, or 3 Pawns v. 1 Pawn. Such end games are fun, and one is disappointed when an opponent gives in too early.

But with passing years we become aware of the importance of end game tactics. We experience our first defeats because of insufficient knowledge of them. We consult a chessbook for beginners, and learn by heart the principles of opposition in pawn endings. That is a dry and boring occupation in contrast with opening variations studied many years before. By experience we learn that our opponents are not easily forced into checkmate. They defend themselves patiently, and leave us with a bad end game, showing us that they are in their element. We understand the ironical saying of the Grandmaster Dr. S. Tartakower, "A game normally consists of three sections; the opening in which you hope to gain the better position, the middle game where you believe you have obtained the better position, and the end game where you know you have a lost game."

The time therefore arrives when we decide to make a closer study of end-game theory. By reading this book you will have shown your interest in the subject, but the author also hopes that you will find the task a pleasant one.

Theo Schuster

Explanation of Symbols and Notation

The 32 pieces and their symbols

No. of pieces	White	Black	
1	♔	♚	
1	♕	♛	
2	♖	♖	♜ ♜
2	♗	♗	♝ ♝
2	♘	♘	♞ ♞
8	♙		♟

The board and the description of the 64 squares

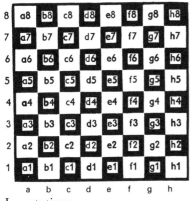

In notation:

K	(King)
Q	(Queen)
R	(Rook)
B	(Bishop)
N	(Knight)

Notation serves the purpose of recording the moves so as to be able to replay them. There is a complete notation and a shortened version.

Here is an example of complete notation from the starting position: 1. e2—e4, e7—e5; 2. Ng1—f3, Nb8—c6; 3. d2—d4; e5 × d4

The first part of the notation tells us White's move, then follows Black's counter-move.

The same moves in the shortened notation:
1. e4, e5; 2. Nf3, Nc6; 3. d4, e × d4
Note that generally only the arrival square is shown, prefaced by the piece symbol.

Where full stops appear after a move number, it indicates a black move. For example, on p. 8 appears the move 8.... Kh8, indicating this was Black's eighth move. White's eighth move appears five lines above it, i.e. 8. h4!

Other symbols used are as follows:

—	moves to
×	takes or captures
+	check
‡	checkmate
0–0	castles on King side
0–0–0	castles on Queen side
!	good move
?	bad move

Notation of a position

The notation of diagram 2 on page 7 is as follows:

Kd2 Qd5 Rd7 Pa5 b2 c2 f2 g2 h3; Kb8 Qb7 Re8 Pa7 b6 c7 f5 g6 h7

The white pieces are indicated first, and then the black pieces.

Major pieces are shown first,

then minor pieces and then the Pawns.

Basic End Game Theory

If a chess game is not completed during the opening or the middle game, then a decision can take place during the end game. As a rule understanding the significance of a material or positional advantage guarantees victory, for example, having two extra Pawns.

Possibilities of combinations do not disappear in the end game, though they lie deeper and are more difficult to recognize. The theory of the chess opening can be learned easily by anybody who cares to study it. Understanding the final end game, however, assumes considerable chess experience and a feeling for the game, as well as extremely conscientious treatment. Every player can acquire these abilities by practice with better players, and above all by studying the games of the masters.

The advantages which we aim for in the end game are not as obvious as in the middle game; the goals at which one first aims are not checkmate and annihilation, but patient siege or ability to outmanoeuvre. Because of the reduction of strength on both sides, the tension, dangers and numerous possibilities no longer exist as in the middle game. Yet the remaining pieces gain a larger field of action as well as more security.

The most important aspect of the end game is the position of the King, and its possible dominance. While the most important piece in chess remains in a safe position during the opening and in the middle game, the King in the end game leaves its relatively safe position, and we soon recognize that it is the most powerful piece left on the board. The kind of move it makes, which gives it the chance to occupy any neighbouring square on its next move, provides this decisive importance.

As a rule therefore, if material balance exists, the side that wins in the end game is the one that has placed the King in the centre, or can break into the opponent's pawn position with the King. The weakness of any pawn structure can be exploited in the end game. An integrated, less weak pawn position is therefore an important factor to aim at in the end game.

How one more Pawn wins

If in a tournament between Masters an end game has developed as in diagram 1, the one with the inferior position generally resigns. The reason is that among players of similar strength, the outcome is quite clear.

The additional white Pawn decides the game, approximately as follows (many roads lead to Rome!):

1. Kf1, Kf8; 2. Ke2, Ke7; 3. Kd3, Kd6;

Do you think it unfair that

1

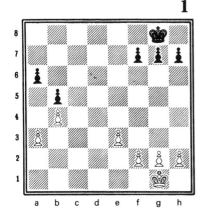

White, in a winning position, should also make the first move? Let White give two moves back just for fun!

4. Kd2, Kd5; 5. Kd3, f5; 6. f3, Ke5; 7. g3, g6; 8. e4, f×e4+; 9. f×e4, g5; 10. g4, h6; (or 10. ... Kf4; 11. h3, Kg3; 12. e5 on the way to queening) 11. Ke3, Ke6; 12. Kd4, Kd6; 13. e5+, Ke6; 14. Ke4, Ke7; 15. Kf5, Kf7; 16. e6+, Ke7; 17. Ke5, Ke8; 18. Kf6, Kf8; 19. e7+, Ke8; 20. Ke6,

Black is compelled to bring about his own checkmate due to *zugzwang*. This term covers those rare positions where there is an advantage to a player simply because his opponent has the move. For example, *see* pp. 32–33.

20. ... a5; 21. b×a5, b4; 22. a6, b×a3; 23. a7, a2; 24. a8 = R ∓

A Queen was not necessary. For those who would like to be even more clever, under-promote to a Bishop: 24. a8 = B,

a1 = Q; Black even gets a Queen as a present, but 25. Bc6 ∓

An elementary example of a different kind:

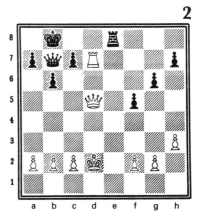

White to move wins!

Materially and positionally, an almost equal position. Only the position of the black Pawns indicates a slight weakness, because on the King's wing the squares f4, g5 and h6 are weakened. The King's wing is always the wing of the King's original position. Seen from White's point of view it is therefore the right half of the board. The Queen's wing is always the left wing, even when the Kings occupy the Queen's wing, as in diagram 2.

The quickest way to win is to exchange off all the pieces, proceeding from diagram 2 as follows: 1. Rd8+, R×d8; 2. Q×d8+, Qc8; 3. Q×c8+, K×c8; 4. Ke3

The white King now moves

quickly on to the King's side in order to get behind the Pawns h7 and g6.

4. ... Kd7; 5. Kf4, Ke6;

Also see variation 5. ... h6 below

6. Kg5, Kf7; 7. Kh6, Kg8; 8. h4!

This is the beginning of the infiltration into the black Pawns' flank, with their subsequent capture.

8. ... Kh8; 9. h5, g × h5; 10. K × h5, Kg7; 11. Kg5 and the f Pawn has to go.

In addition here is the variation, when Black blocks the white King's entry to g5 on the fifth move:

5. ... h6; 6. Ke5!

Now the white King dominates the situation. Black finds himself in *zugzwang* because White has many alternative good moves in reserve as a result of his superior pawn position. Sometimes the possession of one single tempo is sufficient for victory!

6. ... Ke7

Otherwise White wins easily with Kf6, etc.

7. b4!, c6; 8. c4, a6; 9. a4, b5; 10. c × b5, c × b5; 11. a5, h5;

A move which is a last resort by Black, in order to prevent the opposing King penetrating to f6 or d6.

12. h4 *see* diagram 3

White has several alternatives available, and can force the black King to one side depending on which side it yields. White wins easily.

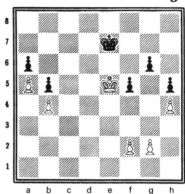

3

Thus White penetrates:

12. ... Kd7; 13. f4, Ke7; 14. g3, Kd7; 15. Kf6, Kd6; 16. K × g6, Kd5; 17. K × f5, Kc4; 18. Kg6, K × b4; 19. f5, Kc3; 20. f6, b4; 21. f7, b3; 22. f8 = Q, b2; 23. Qa3 + , etc.

The easiest way for White is to sacrifice the Queen, and after K × h5 to promote a third Queen with the h or g Pawn.

Using this example, however, we have anticipated the end game theory. Firstly a player has to know pawn endings. In an old chess book I read the following advice, which I am sure will always be valid:

The battle in the end game is almost exclusively for material advantages. Therefore the strategical main rule of the end game is:—endeavour to take more from your opponent than he can take from you, and try to change your Pawns into Queens.

In the end game the player tries

to achieve a passed Pawn, and advance it on to a square on the far side of the board (the opponent's back rank). Often one player will have only one Pawn left, and both players will have to ask themselves: Can the Pawn be promoted, or can the opposing King block the queening square? This brings us to the important principle of achieving the opposition.

The Principle of the Opposition

The attacking King (the one with the Pawn) endeavours to force the opposing King out of opposition; the defending King endeavours not to give up the opposition

How does one maintain the opposition?

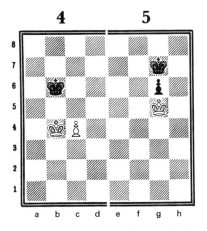

In the positions illustrated in half-diagrams 4 and 5 neither White nor Black can move their respective Pawn on to the last rank, irrespective of whether White or Black moves first.

Allow White to move first in part-diagram 4 on the left:

1. c5 +, Kc6;

Before the Pawn reaches the 6th rank, other moves with the King would be possible for Black, such as . . . Kb7 or . . . Kc7, but the most compelling move is . . . Kc6, as it leaves no choice for White.

2. Kc4, Kc7;

It is wise to keep to the following procedure as a principle: Always retreat with the King in such a way that you can offer "opposition" to your opponent's King—that is, facing the enemy King with an empty square in between them—*near* opposition.

3. Kd5, Kd7;

Near opposition, i.e. with a square in between!

4. c6 +, Kc7; 5. Kc5

Now things are becoming serious for the black King! One wrong move and White will get a passed Pawn on to the queening square. But if Black already knows how to use the opposition, he can easily obtain a draw.

5. . . . Kc8 *see* diagram 6.

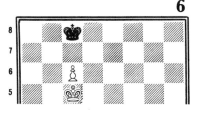

6. Kb6, Kb8!

The black King correctly placed on c8 was ready to move either to the left or to the right with its next move. If White had moved 6. Kd6, then Black would have gone into opposition by 6. ... Kd8!

7. c7 +

Quietly on to the last but one rank!

We can now establish an important principle: If the Pawn moves on to the last but one rank by giving check, a draw is unavoidable. If the Pawn moves quietly on to the last but one rank without giving check, then the Pawn will be promoted. It follows that the game just played must end in a draw.

7. ... Kc8; 8. Kc6 Stalemate—a draw!

Either White gives up the Pawn or produces stalemate. The finish will always be like this, if the defending King maintains the correct opposition.

Now the exercise which is illustrated in the part-diagram 5, where Black moves first:

1. ... Kf7; 2. Kg4, Kf6; 3. Kf4, g5 + ; 4. Kg4, Kg6; 5. Kg3, Kh5;

As yet the moves of the defending King are in no way dictated. Only when the Pawn moves on to the 3rd rank are certain moves necessary for the white King to bring about a draw.

6. Kh3!

Only this move can produce the draw, for after 6. Kg2??, Kg4! the defending King is forced to give up the opposition. Example: *see* diagram 7.

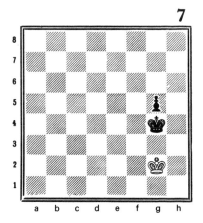

7

In diagram 7 above, whichever way the white King may move, the black King forces it out of opposition: 7. Kg1, then 7. ... Kg3; and the black King has reached the 3rd rank in front of his Pawn! This always means victory! The game would then finish like this: 8. Kh1, Kh3; 9. Kg1, g4; 10. Kh1, g3; 11. Kg1, g2. The Pawn moves *quietly* forward (i.e. without giving check), and thus achieves promotion. 12. Kf2, Kh2; followed by g1 = Q.

But let us go back to the original game before we were sidetracked by diagram 7.

6. ... g4 + ; 7. Kg3,

The alternatives Kh2 or Kg2 also achieve the draw, as we have seen already.

7.... Kg5; 8. Kg2, Kf4;
   An attempt from the other side!
9. Kf2
   Opposition!
9.... g3+ ; 10. Kg2,
   Of course, 10. Kg1 is also adequate 10.... Kf3; 11. Kf1 Opposition! But this is not advisable, for it is always safest to make the move which gives the opponent the least number of alternatives.
10.... Kg4; 11. Kg1 *see* diagram 8
   And whichever side of its Pawn the black King may choose, whether f3 or h3, the white King will be ready to move into opposition.
11.... Kh3; 12. Kh1, Kh4;
   A novel but useless attempt.

13. Kg2, Kg4; 14. Kg1!
   And the sequence can start anew. But according to the rules of chess, it can only last a few moves. Either the same moves are repeated three times over, or the Pawn is lost, or the white King is stalemated. The result is the same in all three cases, namely a draw!

Let us recapitulate what has been learned so far:
1. The defender always tries to be in opposition to the attacker; that is, the defending King does not allow the attacking King to force him from defending the queening square.
2. The attacker must try to reach the 6th rank (or if it is the black King, the 3rd rank) in front of its Pawn.
3. One assumes from the beginning that if the Pawn arrives at the last but one rank by giving check, the outcome will be a draw. But if the Pawn arrives on the last but one rank quietly, without giving check, queening the Pawn will be a foregone conclusion.

The diagonal near-opposition

There is no need to get too worried about the different types of opposition. The German chessmaster, Dr. S. Tarrasch, a great practitioner at the game, once said: "One need know only the typical end games, more is not necessary. From one game to another one has to rely on one's own judgement."

1. Kc5
   This move establishes diagonal opposition to the black King. We can see without difficulty that 1. Kd5? would be useless, because of 1.... Kd7; acquiring the opposition for Black. For this reason we move 1. Kc5! and we have discovered

the strategy of diagonal opposition.

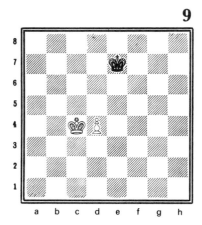

White to move and win...
by the *diagonal* method

1. ... Kd7; 2. Kd5, Kd8; 3. Kd6,
And the rest is well known to us. As we know the principle: King on the 6th rank in front of the Pawn, we can now play blindfolded without making mistakes.

3. ... Ke8;
As we have learned already, logically we should now move Kc7. But let us test our assumptions and continue "wrongly" with—

4. d5, Kd8;
Is Black now in opposition? No! Opposition on the last rank is not possible. White wins, whoever moves! *See* diagram 10

5. Kc6
Equally correct is 5. Ke6

5. ... Kc8; 6. d6, Kd8;

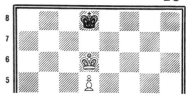

We open our eyes; everything is in order, the Pawn goes on to the 7th rank without giving check.

7. d7, Ke7; 8. Kc7, etc.

Strategies for Queening

If the Pawn moves on to the 7th rank by giving check: only a draw! If it moves on to it without giving check—*quietly*: victory!

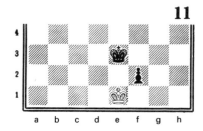

In diagram 11, the Pawn has moved on to the 2nd rank and declared check: the game finishes with stalemate after

1. Kf1, Kf3; stalemate = draw

In diagram 12 the Pawn has moved on to the 2nd rank without giving check: the white King is dislodged from the queening square by

1. Kf2, Kd2;

12

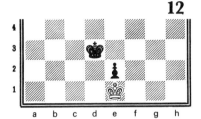

Followed by 2. ... e1 = Q and wins

King on the 6th (3rd) rank in front of its Pawn wins

The opposition cannot operate when the Pawn is on an edge file, and if the defending King can reach the appropriate queening square.

13

14

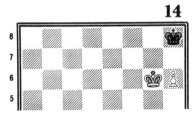

Diagrams 13 and 14—a draw in both cases, regardless of who moves first. Even if in diagram 13 White had five Pawns on the a file (which is possible), none of them could reach the square a8,

because the black King cannot be dislodged from that square. Even the procedure of the *quiet* progress of the Pawn on h6 with 1.h7 is not sufficient (as in cases with Pawns on files b to g). The black King is only stalemated.

Here are further examples to demonstrate the near-opposition:

15

A draw, White or Black to move

When White moves
1. Ke4,
Black moves into opposition with
1. ... Ke6!
If white moves 1. Kf4, Black still gains the opposition by 1. ... Kf6! In the case of 1. f4, Black can still force a draw by moving to e6, f6 or even g6.

But let us suppose that after
1. Ke4,
Black makes a defensive error by moving
1. ... Kf6?;

13

We can now see how Black has given up the opposition.

2. Kf4, Kf7; 3. Kf5, Kf8; 4. Kf6!

White has now reached a typical winning position, for the procedures in Pawn end games indicate that promotion is certain when the attacking King reaches the 6th (3rd) rank in front of its Pawn: and that is the case here—see diagram 16

16

A win for White no matter who moves first!

4. ... Kg8; 5. f4, Kf8; 6. f5, Ke8; 7. Kg7 (or if 6. ... Kg8; then 7. Ke7)
And the Pawn forces its way to promotion.

Do not hurry your moves in the end game, especially when there is only one Pawn left on the board. Every move will be important in deciding whether the game will end in a victory or a draw!

Therefore in diagram 17 do not move 1. c4?, for Black would be able to force a draw by 1. ... Kc5;

(and even with 1. ... Ka7). But with the correct move:

1. Kb4,
Black is compelled to give up the opposition

1. ... Kc6; 2. Kc4, Kc7; 3. Kc5, etc.

Four test cases

17   18

White to move wins
Black to move, a draw

White to move, a draw
Black to move wins

Equally, White to move wins with:

1. Kc4, Kc6; 2. c3 (a waiting move!)
And the black King must give up the opposition, e.g.

2. ... Kc7; 3. Kc5, Kb7; (if 3. ... Kc8; 4. Kc6, and Black must give way all the same)

4. Kd6, Kb6; 5. c4, Kb7; 6. c5, Kc8; *see* diagram 19
Now not the hurried move

19

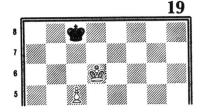

7.c6?? for 7....Kd8; a draw. But applying the two principles:
1. Move on to the last but one rank without giving check (which would happen after 6.c6, Kd8; 7.c7+)
2. Move the King on to the 6th rank in front of the Pawn!

The correct move is:

7.Kc6, "Give up the opposition!"
7....Kb8; 8.Kd7, etc. or analogously
7....Kd8; 8.Kb7, etc.

If in diagram 17, Black is to move first, the black King will achieve the opposition with:
1....Kb5! and for example 2.Kc3, Kc5; 3.Kd3, Kd5;
    And White will not be able to make progress. The white King is able to get in front of its Pawn, but *not on to the 6th rank in front of its Pawn!*
1....Kc5?? would be quite wrong as a first move, for after
2.Kc3!, Kc6; 3.Kc4, etc., and we know already that the black King will have to give up the opposition.

Watch out for the stalemate trap!

The stalemate situation appears in many end games. The stalemate trap is the last refuge for the defender, and the attacker must be on his guard.

In pawn endings the following positions are suspect:

20

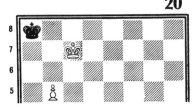

White to move: 1.b6? Stalemate!

21

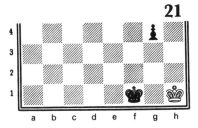

Black to move: 1....g3?
Stalemate!

For diagram 20 the correct move would be:
1.Kb6, Kb8; 2.Ka6,
    Only that move will win, for the black King must be dislodged from the stalemate square a7. Also 2.Kc6, Ka7! 3.b6+, Ka8!; ruins the chance of a win for White.
Alternatively 3.Kc7 (instead of 3.b6+?) 3....Ka8; 4.Kb6 allows White to return to the winning path.
2....Ka8; 3.b6, Kb8; 4.b7, etc.
    In diagram 21, the move 1....g3

15

would also lead to stalemate, therefore:

1.... Kf2; 2. Kh2, g3 +,

As the white King no longer controls the queening square b8, Black does not need preparations like 2.... Kf3; 3. Kh1, Kg3, etc. but can move straight towards his objective:

3. Kh1, g2 + ; followed by g1 = Q, etc.

The Distant Opposition

The simple position, which we know already from diagram 15, illustrates well why we ought to know something about distant opposition. *See* diagram 22

22

Black to move forces a draw!

Certainly a draw will only be achieved by a player who is fully conversant with the tactics of distant opposition. Black must work out, even before he makes the first move, that he will be able to move on to the correct squares after the white King's countermove.

This is how it looks:

1.... Ke7!;

Every other move is a loser. Examples: a) 1.... Ke6?; 2. Ke4, Kf6; 3. Kf4, and Black must give up the opposition, the result of which we know. Or b) 1.... Kf6?; 2. Kf4, with the same position as in a).

Or c) 1.... Kg6?; 2. Ke4! diagonal opposition! 2.... Kf6; 3. Kf4, and for the third time the black King must give up the opposition.

But after the only correct move 1.... Ke7; White is powerless, for Black holds the key to all three oppositions—near, distant or diagonal—just as White would like to play it.

2. Ke4, Ke6; or

2. Kf4, Kf6; or

2. f4, which is useless, as Black will be able to gain a draw by moving the King along the 6th rank—... Kd6; ... Ke6; ... Kf6; without hindrance.

Just for practice, consider a similar example in diagram 23.

(a) With which move does Black obtain a draw?

(b) Can White to move win?

Now rearrange the position in diagram 23, placing the white Pawn on c3, and the black King on c7. Try out two other exercises:

16

23

(a) With Black to move, how should he play?

(b) Can White to move win?

The importance of knowing about distant opposition was brought home to me during the German Chess Championships in 1948. Up until then I knew about it from hearsay; but an incident here really enlightened me. The starting position was as follows:

Th. Sch. (White): Kg2 Rf5 Pa2 f3 g4

Sahlmann (Black): Kd5 Re5 Pa5 g5

That 1.Kg3?, R × f5!; 2.g × f5, Ke5; 3.Kg4, Kf6; 4.f4, g × f4 + ; 5.Kf4, would lead only to a draw was well known to me. (We are going to learn about the strategy of the confinement at the sides later on!)

Certain of victory, I therefore moved:

1. R × e5 + , Ke5; 2. a4, in order to win easily as follows, 2....Kd4;

3. Kf2, Ke5; 4. Ke3, Kf6; 5. Kd4, Ke6; 6. Ke4, etc.

But to my astonishment the Master from Hamburg moved:

2. ... Ke6!! achieving distant opposition.

The game could no longer be won. *See* diagram 24.

An expensive apprenticeship

24

Schuster v. Sahlmann after ... Ke6!!

So as to understand what follows, one must know that the establishment of a passed Pawn with the move f4 leads ultimately to the confinement of the white King along the left hand edge of the board. But more about that later.

From diagram 24 the game developed like this:

3. Kf2, Kf6!; 4. Ke2, Ke6; 5. Kd2, Kd6; 6. Kc2, Kc6; 7. Kb3, Kd5; 8. Kc2, Kc6; 9. Kd1, Kd7;

Believe it or not—every other move by the black King loses!

Test: 9. Kd1, Kd6?; 10. Kd2!, Kc5; 11. Ke3, Kd5; 12. Kd3, victory! Or 11. Ke3, Kb4; in order to free the black a Pawn to advance. 12. f4, g × f4 + ; 13. K × f4, K × a4; 14. g5, Kb4; (On moving Kb3 Black gets into check from the white Queen appearing on g8!) 15. g6, a4; 16. g7, a3; 17. g8 = Q, etc.

White then tried for a little while the tactics of distant opposition, but Black kept in step:

10. Kc1, Kc7; 11. Kb2, Kd6; 12. Kc2,

And then White moved once more to g2 with the King, Black opposing accordingly, and the Championship Hall in Essen was celebrating a sensation. For the spectators were whispering to each other: "What extraordinary moves these two are putting together . . .!"

An expensive apprenticeship indeed for my first German Chess Championship. When dealing with Bähr's study on page 22, we will refer back to the question why White from the starting position in diagram 24, could never succeed with the move f4. The resultant pawn ending with white Pawn on a4, and black Pawn on a5 is elementary—even if it is known only to the experts.

The Rule of the Square

Irrespective of whether the black King is on a3 or a8, is it able to

25

Black to move: a draw

catch the passed Pawn on its journey to the 8th rank? There is no need for us to count, but simply to construct a square mentally, which reaches from the Pawn's position to the queening square. In the case of Pg3, the square is formed by the sides g3–g8/g3–b3/b3–b8/b8–g8.

The rule of the square tells us: If the King succeeds in reaching one of the squares within the big square, then the Pawn can be caught—a draw.

The Test:

1. ... Kb3; 2. g4, Kc4;

Please note that the "square" gets smaller with every move. Now it is circumscribed by g4–g8/g4–c4/c4–c8/c8–g8. The black King stands on one of the squares within the big square!

3. g5, Kd5; 4. g6, Ke6; 5. g7, Kf7;

And the Pawn is caught.

If we start with the black King on the square a8, we get the same result: (1. ... Kb8 or ... Kb7).

26

Black to move reaches the square

Consider diagram 26. The next move by White will quite obviously involve the a Pawn advancing two squares. Can Black to move still catch it? The rule of the square provides the answer quickly. The square looks like this: a4–a8/a4–e4/ e4–e8/e8–a8. We are only interested in whether the black King, starting from g2 can get to the near corner, that is e4, in time. Yes, the King will do it, with:

1. ... Kf3; 2. a4, Ke4;

And they will meet each other on square b7!

The Outside Passed Pawn

Every player knows that a Pawn which has no opposing Pawn on its way to the queening square, is called a passed Pawn. But what is an *outside passed Pawn*? While still a teenager, and playing with the chess club in Stuttgart, I was given my first end game lesson by Dr.

Lörbroks, an old and friendly judge from Leipzig. He put before me the following position in diagram 27.

27

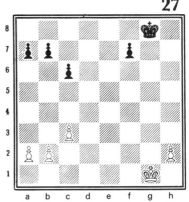

No matter who moves first,
White wins!

Both sides have, apart from their three Pawns each on the Queen's side, a passed Pawn still in its original position. In spite of the fact that all other positions seem to balance each other (neither King is in the centre), White will be the automatic winner of the end game.

The key to the secret is to be found in the *outside passed Pawn*; that is, the passed Pawn which is furthest away from the centre—in this case the white Pawn on h2!

While sooner or later the black King has to catch the white Pawn on the h file, White takes the black Pawn on the f file. This means that White is closer by two files to the remaining Pawns, which he takes one by one, leaving finally one white Pawn.

In practice it looks like this:

1. ... Kg7; 2. Kg2, Kg6; 3. Kf3, Kg5; 4. Kg3, Kh5; 5. c4, Kg5; 6. h4+, Kh5; 7. Kh3, f5;

If Black moves the Pawns on the Queen's side, they will be the white King's victims even more quickly.

8. Kg3, c5; 9. b3, b6;

The moves leading up to the decisive action on the King's side are as good as exhausted.

10. Kf4, K × h4; 11. K × f5, Kg3;

The situation on that side is now cleared up; the Kings are now hurrying to the Pawns on the other side. But the head start of the white King is too much, for the black King is always one file behind in the race, due to having to capture the *outside passed Pawn*.

12. Ke5, Kf3; 13. Kd5, Ke3; 14. Kc6, Kd3; 15. Kb7, Kc3; 16. K × a7, Kb2; 17. K × b6, K × a2; 18. K × c5, K × b3; 19. Kb5, etc.

The knowledge of this practical rule is extremely important in chess. Once you remember it, you can solve the later puzzles without difficulties:

An exercise

Again White has the outside passed Pawn, but there are still Rooks in the game, and we cannot rely yet on an automatic victory during the pawn ending.

But White sees that after the disappearance of the Rooks, it will be

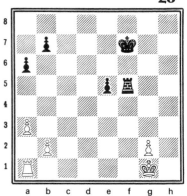

28

White to move wins!

the outside passed Pawn that will guarantee victory.

Therefore quickly:

1. Rf1!, Rf4!; 2. g3!

Forces Black to exchange now or later. On the other hand no passed Pawn would exist after 2. Rf4+?, e × f4.

2. ... Rf6; 3. R × f6+, K × f6; 4. Kf2,

Here is the approximate development of the game for the less accomplished player:

4. ... Kf5; 5. Kf3, e4+; 6. Ke3, Ke5; 7. g4, b6; 8. b3, a5; 9. a4, (9. b4 also wins, but a4 is more exact) 9. ... Kd5; 10. g5, Ke5; 11. g6, Kf6; 12. K × e4, K × g6; 13. Kd5,

And the white King takes both the black Pawns

The rule, which the friendly old judge explained, allows us to recognize and to solve the following puzzles:

Puzzle No. 1

29

White to move wins!

Puzzle No. 2

30

Black to move wins!

A first glance may prompt the question: "Where do I find the outside passed Pawn?" Look carefully and you will see that it can be created.

The solutions to the puzzles are on page 64 at the end of the book.

The Confinement at the Side

At about the same time as Dr. Lörbroks gave me his first lesson on the outside passed Pawn, I was confronted with the following end game position during a tournament.

However, hopes of victory, based on the passed Pawn on h7 were misplaced.

31

Black to move

This is what happened:

1. ... Kf5; 2. Kg3, a5; 3. a4, Kg5;
4. f4+, Kf5; 5. Kf3, h6; 6. Kg3,
h5; 7. Kh4, K×f4; 8. K×h5, Ke4;

I did not know then that victory was impossible with the outside passed Pawn when the remaining Pawns are positioned on a4 and a5! This results in the well known confinement—of which I knew nothing at the time.

9. Kg4, Kd4; 10. Kf4, Kc4;
11. Ke4, Kb4; 12. Kd4, K×a4;
13. Kc4, Ka3; 14. Kc3, Ka2;

21

15. Kc2, a4; 16. Kc1, a3; 17 Kc2, Ka1; 18. Kc1, a draw. *See* diagram 32.

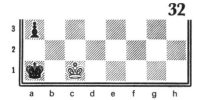

32

Confinement with stalemate

The black King could have avoided the confinement of this position. On the 15th move (White Kc2, Black Ka3 Pa5), Black could have avoided the confinement of his King by 15.... Kb4 instead of 15.... a4. But then we know already that the white King could move on to the corner square a1, and an edge file Pawn cannot win when the opposing King occupies the queening square.

The outcome of the end position in the diagram above is either the repetition of the moves ...Ka2; Kc2, or a draw by stalemate after the black Pawn moves to a2.

The outcome of end games are difficult to predict. World Champion Dr. E. Lasker expressed it sceptically like this: "It is not possible to predict a win, draw or loss in an end game if the material advantage is not at least a whole Rook." This exaggeration of Lasker's of course excludes those positions which are procedural certainties, including those where one Pawn more is sufficient for victory.

Sense deception?

Comparison of two similar positions which may deceive eye and mind:

No matter who moves first, can White win in either of the two positions shown below in diagrams 33 and 34?

If your answer is in the affirm-

Study—W. Bähr 1936

33

Schuster v. Sahlmann
End of game in German
Championship, 1948

34

ative, in which of the two positions does White win?

Is this a catch question, you may think. It makes no difference whether the judgement is to be made by an amateur or an expert.

It is quite clear that if one of the two positions can be won—that position is most likely *where the passed Pawn is furthest from the field of action* (Pawns a4/a5).

What a deception of the senses, where logic is apparently turned upside down. But the reader will remember that White, in the position of diagram 34, with the favourably placed passed Pawn, was unable to win (*see* p. 22).

First the solution which we ought to play through: *see* diagram 33

1. Kd4!, Kf5; 2. Kc4, Kf4; 3. Kb5, Ke5; 4. K × a5, Kd6; 5. Kb6 wins

The black King is kept away from the square which would initiate the confinement of the white King, after

5. ... Kd7; 6. Kb7. No problems so far.

Now diagram 34:

1. Ke4, Kg5;

The result would be unchanged even if White moves first with his King on f6, Pg6 and Black's King on f8 (please try).

2. Kd4, K × g4;

Although the black King is now one file further away from the field of action than in the previous example, he saves the game by having time to reach square c8! Impossible?

3. Kc4, Kf5; 4. Kb5, Ke6; 5. K × a5, Kd7; 6. Kb6, Kc8!

The King has done it! The end is the confinement of the white King on a7/a8 (after 7. Ka7, Kc7).

But now it is time to explain the "deception of the senses". Logic is not contradicted by the fact that the passed Pawn in this latter case does not guarantee a win, whilst in the previous example with the Pawn on file f it does; simply because the white King too is closer to the black Pawn on a5!

The German end game amateur W. Bähr established in 1936 the rule of the Pawns which will win, when associated with opposing Pawns on a4/a5:

Passed Pawns outside the diagonal c7–h2 do not guarantee a win.

This was something which I found difficult to believe in 1948. But as mentioned previously, at that time I avoided the variation which I thought involved confinement and a draw.

Confinement at the edge of the board is part of a chess player's staple diet. But even here, the Masters are sometimes wrong.

Giving in too early

The Bavarian Master and great end game expert Dr. Rödl had just moved h4—h5—diagram 35, whereupon his opponent after long consideration, resigned. But once again a game was abandoned too early. Black had not recognized the finer points of confinement theory:

Dr. Rödl v. Röhrich
German Championship 1947

35

Black to move—gave in!

1. ...g × h5; 2.g × h5, f5! 3.d5+, c × d5; 4.c × d5+, Kd6; 5.Kf5, K × d5; 6.K × f6, Kd6; 7.Kg6, Ke6; 8.K × h6, Kf6; 9.Kh7, Kf7; 10.h6,

Black now has to give up the confinement.

10. ...Kf8; 11.Kg6, Kg8; 12.Kf6, Kh7; 13.Ke6, K × h6; 14.Kd6, *see* diagram 36

The distance between the two Kings is three squares: "Isn't the journey from file h too far?" No! For the second time, confinement is possible

14. ...Kg6; 15.Kc6, Kf7; 16.Kb5, Ke7; 17.K × a5, Kd7 (or Kd8); 18.Kb6, Kc8; 19.Ka7, Kc7; 20.a5, Kc8 (or Kc6); 21.a6, Kc7; 22.Ka8, Kc8;

The second confinement

The second confinement is complete, thus a draw! Well,

36

that would have been nice! But Black unfortunately surrendered because he undervalued the resources of the defence!

The Use of Triangulation

There are situations in the end game where each side is in possession of one Pawn, but no passed Pawn, and where a win is still possible. It can be achieved by using the rule of triangulation.

First of all, in diagram 37, we notice that Black could easily achieve a draw without his Pawn on c6. Only the possession of this Pawn prevents him from doing so. The reason for this is the black King's inability to move on to a suitable opposition square, from which he would have to face the white King in order to achieve a draw.

1. ...Kd7; 2.Kf5, Ke7; 3.Ke5, Kd7; 4.Kf6, Kd8; 5.Ke6, Kc7;

37

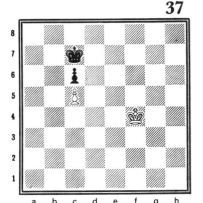

White wins, no matter who starts

6. Ke7, Kc8; 7. Kd6, Kb7; 8. Kd7 and wins.

The Pawn on c6 is lost, which creates the pre-condition for winning, i.e. King in front of the Pawn, on the 6th rank.

White made use of the triangle e7–d6–d7. If Black moves straight away to the other side, then White will use the triangle e5–e6–d6. One can see this as follows:

1.... Kb7; 2. Ke5, Ka6; 3. Ke6! *see* diagram 38.

Black would reverse the roles if White had made the wrong move 3. Kd6? For there follows

38

3.... Kb5! and Black gains the Pawn on c5, winning the game.

3.... Ka5, 4. Kd7,

Now it is the triangle e6–d7–d6

4.... Kb5; 5. Kd6 and wins.

The black King cannot maintain the protection of the Pawn on c6. We also know that Black's opposition by Kc8 against White's Kc6 will be of no consequence, because King in front of its Pawn, on the 6th rank always wins.

39

White obtains a draw

See diagram 39 above. After 1. Kd2?, c4!; 2. c3, Kb3; White would lose the Pawn without being able to obtain the position with his King, from which to achieve the draw. 1. Kd2?, c4; 2. Kd1, c3; also results in a loss. But a draw can be achieved if we remember the principle of the opposition:

1. c4!, Kb3; 2. Kc1 (or Kd2), Kc4; 3. Kc2!

Opposition and a draw! White

25

has managed to avoid the utilization of the triangle, by moving his Pawn on to the 4th rank.

Puzzle No. 3

40

White to move: how does it end?

White will lose the Pawn on c5. We have already learned so much about the opposition in pawn endings, that if we count the moves, we can make a firm prediction. Although White loses the Pawn, can he still obtain a draw? Solution on page 64.

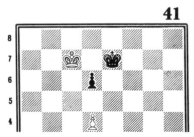

41

White to move wins
Black to move obtains a draw

In diagram 41 it is not difficult to see that White wins with

1. d5 and 2. K × d6

Black to move and draw is achieved by

1. ... d5! 2. Kc6, Ke6; 3. Kc5, Ke7! (and not 3. ... Kd7??; 4. K × d5 at which point the black King must relinquish the opposition)

4. K × d5, Kd7;

Opposition and a draw! Of course Black could also draw with 1. ... Ke6; 2. Kc6, d5; but the direct route with 1. ... d5! is the most correct and efficient one.

King and two Pawns

If King and one Pawn wins frequently, surely King + 2 Pawns must always win? Yes, usually, but as diagram 42 shows, prudence is still essential. With Black to move first it would be easy;

42

White wins

1.…Kb8; 2.b7, Ka7; 3.Kc7, etc.
    With White to move first, we
have to beware of pitfalls:
1.b7+, Kb8; 2.b5, Ka7;
    A stalemate trap would now
be 3.Kc7? A draw! Therefore
gently and with cunning give
up one of the Pawns in order to
achieve the theoretically well-
known winning position.
3.b8 = Q+!, K × b8; 3.Kb6,
    The rest we know from what
we have learned so far, the b
Pawn gains promotion on the
8th rank.

The Pawn Breakthrough

Every player will come across
the position shown in diagram 43
at one time or another. It is the
oldest example of the pawn breakthrough:
1.b6!, a × b6; 2.c6, b × c6; 3.a6,

43

And the Pawn is on its way
to being promoted.

44

H. Müller v. Svacina,
Vienna 1941

Or:
1.b6, c × b6; 2.a6!, b × a6;
    This time the c Pawn becomes
a passed Pawn.
3.c6, etc.

Diagram 44 illustrates an end
game where the value of knowing
theory can be seen clearly. It is
obvious that neither side can win,
for White has only to move Ke1,
Ke2, Ke1, etc. Black also realizes
that his King, which had pen-
etrated well, would not be able
to achieve anything, and therefore withdraws:
1.…Kc4; 2.Kc2, Kb5; 3.Kb3,
Kc6; 4.Kb4, Kd6;
    Black tempts the white King,
and White now believes he can
win by the use of triangulation.
5.Kb5, Kd7; 6.Kc5, Ke6; 7.Kc6,
g4; 8.Kc5,
    White now believes he has
achieved his goal. If there is any
"law-abiding" justice in this

world, White must win when he takes the d Pawn. But this is precisely what Black intended his opponent to do.

A splendid pawn-break-through decides the game:

8. ... f4!!; 9. e × f4,

Not 9. g × f4, for then the h Pawn gets through.

9. ... h4!;

Threatening ... h3;

10. g × h4, g3!; 11. f × g3, e3;

On its way to being promoted. *See* diagram 45.

Although Black has one Bishop more, the white Pawns are successful in breaking through to the 8th rank:

1. a6, b × a6; 2. b × c6,

And c7/c8 = Q cannot be stopped.

45

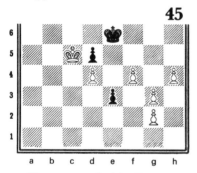

The group of white Pawns
is useless!

But Black has other options for his defence:

1. a6, d5!

Now, neither a × b7, b × c6 nor c × d5 will be successful because of ... Bf4! when Black

46

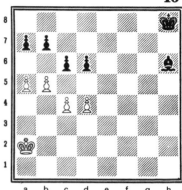

White to move wins!

controls the squares c7/b8. However there is a second way through:

2. b6!!

A white Queen is gained in two moves on square a8, whatever Black's counter moves, e.g. 2. ... b × a6; 3. b × a7, or 2. ... a × b6; 3. a7, etc.

A simple breakthrough with Pawns can be illustrated with the following position: White—Pf5 h5; Black—Pf7 g7.

White wins with:

1. f6, g × f6; 2. h6, etc.

Black to move achieves a draw with:

1. ... f6!

Queen Against Pawn on the 7th Rank

Queen always wins against a Pawn on the 7th rank supported by a King, except for the Rook and Bishop Pawns! Thus black Pawns on b2, d2, e2 and g2 always lose. A draw can be achieved by the edge Pawns on a2 and h2, and the Pawns on c2 and f2.

The white Queen takes the Pawn by playing the following characteristic moves:

1. Qd4 +, Kf1; 2. Qf4 +, Kg2; 3. Qe3,

The typical tactic—the Queen forces the King to block the queening square.

3. ... Kf1; 4. Qf3 +, Ke1; 5. Kb7, The King's first step towards the field of action.

that the black King + Pawn take up the same position three times, because on each occasion the white King is on a different square. The rule which would allow Black to claim a draw, namely the repetition of the same position on three occasions, includes the requirement that *all pieces* are on the same squares three times.

This winning route, with the use of the King, is of no avail when dealing with the Rook and Bishop Pawns because of the saving grace of a stalemate by the weaker side. *See* diagram 48.

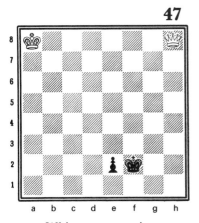

47

White to move wins

48

A draw

5. ... Kd2; 6. Qf2, Kd1; 7. Qd4 +, Kc2; 8. Qe3, Kd1; 9. Qd3 +, Ke1; 10. Kc6, Kf2; 11. Qd2, Kf1; 12. Qf4 +, Kg2; 13. Qe3, Kf1; 14. Qf3 +, Ke1; 15. Kd5,

This will probably be sufficient to demonstrate the road to victory.

By the way, it does not matter

1. Qd4 +, Ka2; 2. Qc3, Kb1; 3. Qb3 +, Ka1!; 4. Q × c2, stalemate.

A draw is achieved, too, when an edge Pawn is involved. *See* diagram 49.

1. Qb3, Ka1;

A draw because the white King is too far away.

49

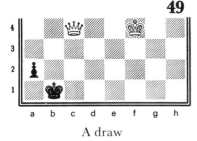

A draw

Winning area v. an edge Pawn

The dotted line (Fig. 50) indicates the winning area of the edge Pawn. If the attacking King is within that area, the Pawn cannot achieve a draw:

1.Qd1 + , Kb2; 2.Qd2 + , Kb1;
3.Kb4, a1 = Q; 4.Kb3,

Black cannot prevent checkmate in spite of his Queen.

The reader may test that a win is not possible if the white King starts on a square outside the winning area, e.g. e5.

50

White to move wins!

Winning area v. a Bishop's Pawn

A win by the Queen is only possible if the white King is already within the winning area, i.e. the dotted line.

1.Qb8 + , Ka2; 2.Qa7 + , Kb2;
3.Qd4 + , Kb1; 4.Qb4 + , Ka1 (or Ka2); 5.Kd2,
or 4....Kc1; 5.Qa3 + , etc.

51

White to move wins

If we alter diagram 51, by placing the white King on a4, the following will happen:

1.Qb8 + , Ka1; 2.Kb3, c1 = Q;
3.Qa7 + , Kb1; 4.Qa2 ǂ

If instead we alter diagram 51, by placing the white King on b4, it will look like this:

1.Qh7, Kb2; 2.Qh2, Kb1 (or Ka1); 3.Kb3, c1 = Q; 4.Qa2 ǂ

Polerio's corner-game

The player with the white pieces, the U.S. Grandmaster J. Kashdan, who received a special prize for

Kashdan v. Flohr, Hamburg 1930

52

White to move wins

this end game, had carefully pre-calculated the end by means of Polerio's corner-game.

If one counts all the moves necessary for promotion of both sides, one realizes that both will gain a Queen in the same time.

Up to e8 = Q, White will need four moves. Black equally needs four moves. But we can work out

53

beforehand that Black, after 1.Kf5, h4; 2.e6, h3; 3.e7, h2; 4.e8 = Q, h1 = Q; 5.Qa8 + ! will lose his Queen straight away. *See* diagram 53.

For this reason Black will have to lose one move in order to get his King from f3 to g2. The first moves of the two Grandmasters were therefore as follows:

1.Kf5, h4; 2.e6, h3; 3.e7, h2; 4.e8 = Q, Kg2; 5.Kg4!, Black resigned.

To Flohr this was a foregone conclusion, for the end would have been 5.... h1'= Q; 6.Qe2 +

54

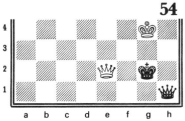

The Italian G. Polerio discovered in 1590 how this position (diagram 54)—for Black an unfavourable corner position—can be won by White:

6....Kg1; 7.Kg3!

Threatening mate in one, so 7....Qf3 + ; 8.K × f3 wins.

Not 8.Q × f3? stalemate.

White could have gone for a draw with 1.Kf4!, but he wanted to force the issue, and in consequence lost the game:

1.Kg6?, Ke4; 2.R × h5, R × h5; 3.K × h5,

The Pawn is captured and both sides obtain a Queen on

successive moves. But White did not remember the fateful end of Polerio's corner-game.

Dr. Antze v. Elstner
German Championship 1934

55

White to move, lost!

3. ... Kf5!; 4. Kh6, d5; 5. h5, d4;
6. Kg7, d3; 7. h6, d2; 8. h7, d1 = Q;
9. h8 = Q, Qd7 + ; White resigned.

56

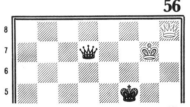

The end would have been like this:

(a) 10. Kf8, Qd8 + !; 11. Kg7, Qe7 + ; 12. Kg8, Kg6!; or
(b) 10. Kh6, Qd6 + , 11. Kg7,
    If 11. Kh7, then ... Qg6 ⧾ or 11. Kh5, then ... Qg6 + followed by ... Qg4 ⧾.

11. ... Qe7 + ; 12. Kh6, Qg5 + ;
13. Kh7, Qg6 ⧾

In no way could White's King and Queen escape the checkmate in the corner position.

The magician "Zugzwang"

Zugzwang is an important concept in the end game. A decisive disadvantage may arise for one player simply because it is his turn to move.

57

Whoever moves first, wins.

Black to move wins with

1. ... Kd5!

    White is in *zugzwang*! Only because White has to move now does the black King achieve penetration into White's camp.

White to move wins in the same way with:

1. Kd4!

    Black is forced to allow White a clear path with

1. ... Kc6; 2. Ke5

    Or with 1. ... Ke6; 2. Kc5.

    Black could win in a contemptuous way, by moving the King on to the Queen's wing and taking the

58

Black obtains a new Queen

two Pawns a3/b4, while White has to cope with the h Pawn. But the magician *zugzwang* achieves much quicker results:

1. Kg1, h2 + ; 2. Kh1, Kh3 !

> White in *zugzwang* has to move his Pawns.

3. a4, b × a4; 4. b5, a3 !

> Certainly not 4. ... a × b5? for White would be stalemated.

5. b × a6 (or b6), a2; 6. a7, a1 = R ∓

The Italian Chessmaster G. Polerio published as far back as 1585, a rather witty position which illustrates the magic of *zugzwang*.

Probably 99 per cent of chess-players are convinced that White can win with the methods of the average player, who is not conversant with end game procedures. Namely with: 1. Rg1, a1 = Q; (or 1. Rc2 +, Kb1; 2. R × a2, etc.); 2. R × a1, K × a1; 3. Ke3, Kb2; 4. Kf4, Kc3; 5. Kg5, Kd4; 6. K × g6, Ke5; 7. K × h5, Kf5;

59

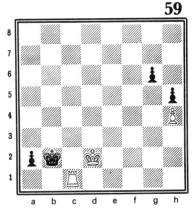

White to move wins

We know in advance that White cannot win because of the confinement of the King at the side.

The Master, however, knows the route to success, which is rather unusual, because a Rook has to be sacrificed:

1. Ra1, K × a1;

> If 1. ... Ka3; 2. Kc3, etc.

2. Kc2 !

> The magic formula of *zugzwang* automatically achieves checkmate.

2. ... g5; 3. h × g5, h4; 4. g6, h3; 5. g7, h2; 6. g8 = Q, h1 = Q; 7. Qg7 ∓ !

Rook Endings
Rook and Pawn v. Rook

As far back as 1777 the French Chessmaster A. Philidor showed that this position ends with a draw. Rule: When the defending King dominates the queening square of the passed Pawn (which can be advanced as far as the fifth rank),

60

A drawn position by Philidor
and the defending Rook stands on
the 6th rank, the game ends in a
draw.

In diagram 60 both conditions
are met: (a) the black King dominates the queening square of the
Pawn (e8), and (b) the defending
Rook is on the 6th rank.

The black Rook moves along
the 6th rank—always a long way
away from the white King, on the
squares a6, b6 and c6—until the
Pawn moves on to the 6th rank.
Only then is the strategy changed:
1....Ra6; 2.e5, Rb6; 3.Ra7, Rc6;
4.e6, Rc1; 5.Kf6, Rf1 + ; a draw.

The black Rook can give
check continuously, or alternatively White gives up his Pawn.

An ending which occurs daily.
Black wins because White has in-
correctly defended:

1....f3; 2.Ra1 (countering the
threat of ...Rb1 ≠).

2....Rh2; 3.Kg1, f2 + ; 4.Kf1,
Rh1 + ;

61

Black wins

And White now loses the
Rook.

Reverting back to the original
position in diagram 61, if we
suppose that the white Rook had
come from a8 in moving 1.Ra3 +,
then it can be seen that White
could have obtained a draw by the
alternative move 1.Rg8 + . There
would follow 1....Kf3; 2.Kg1,
Rb1 + ; 3.Kh2.

In attack and defence, *the Rooks
always belong behind the Pawns*!

"Behind your own as well as
behind the opposition Pawns"—
thus goes the old maxim that
Tarrasch taught the chess world.

A standard example

White to move has the choice of
supporting his passed Pawn *with
Ra8? from the front*, or *with Rd2
from behind*.

If White moves 1.Ra8?, Black
moves straightaway with ...Re2 +
and ...Ra2 behind White's passed

62

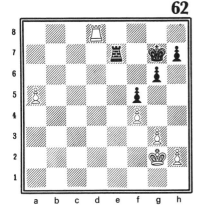

Pawn, and the game is drawn. Subsequent moves by the white Pawn reduce, by one rank on each occasion, the effective range of the Rook on a8.

If, however, White chooses the correct strategy of:

1. Rd2 followed by Ra2, his Rook gains more space whenever the passed Pawn moves forward, The hiding place at a7.

63

White wins

and at the same time limits the black Rook more and more in its passive position.

Be warned of a common error regarding the edge Pawns—*see* diagram 63. White has to keep the square a7 in reserve for his King, and therefore must avoid moving prematurely to a7 with his Pawn.

Although the defending Rook has taken up the favourable position—behind the Pawn, does White win?
1. Kc5, Kf7; 2. Kb6, Rb1 + ;
3. Ka7, Ke7; 4. Rb8, Ra1; 5. Kb7, Rb1 + ; 6. Ka8, Ra1; 7. a7, Kd7; 8. Kb7, Rb1 + ; 9. Ka6, Ra1 + ; 10. Kb6, Rb1 + ; 11. Kc5.

The white King moves towards the black Rook when in check, and ...a8 = Q follows.

The skewer

64

A draw

The position in diagram 64 is a draw, if Black defends himself correctly and uses his Rook to cut off the white King from the 5th rank. But there is an important tactical device which the defender has to remember in this and other similar Rook endings: the possibility of a skewer! After—
1. a7?,

35

Black must not move closer with his King, e.g. 1....Ke7?; because White then starts his threat of a skewer with 2.Rh8!, threatening a8=Q. If 2....R×a7; 3.Rh7+, and the black Rook is lost. The correct move is:

1....Kg7!

Avoiding the skewer, and holding the drawn position.

The tactical use of the skewer was also the climax of an ending in Budapest 1946:

Black to move can also win by other means, but most quickly by this strategy:

1....Ra1+; 2.K×e2, a2!;

White has nothing to offer

Dr. Euwe v. Rethy

65

against the threat of 3....Rh1; threatening ...a1; thus after·

3.K×e2, Rh1; 4.R×a2, Rh2+

During the Grandmaster Championship in New York 1927, the future world champion discovered

Dr. Alekhine v. Spielmann

66

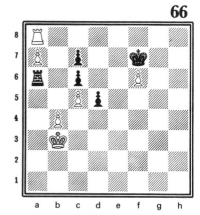

White to move

a winning variation. Playing with White in this Rook ending, he moved:

1.b5!, c×b5; 2.Kb4!

Already at this stage victory is clearly visible, because Black cannot afford the protecting move 2....c6; as there is the threat of a skewer by 3.Rh8! A move by the c Pawn would clear the 7th rank, and after 3....R×a7; 4.Rh7+, the black Rook would be lost.

Spielmann resigned because after 2.Kb4, if 2....d4; 3.K×b5, Ra1; 4.Kc4 wins.

Note that Black could not take the Pawn on f6, because of Rf8+ followed by a8=Q.

Bridge building

What the Italian Master, Lucena, already knew about Rook endings in 1497, is by no means known to all chess players today.

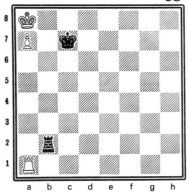

White wins   A draw

Bridge building can be used in almost all similar positions to that in diagram 67, except with the Rook Pawns. White wins like this:

1. Rg1 +, Kh7; 2. Rg4!

Bridge building should take place on the 4th rank, not on the 5th, as is believed by some players, though one can also win in this laborious way.

2. ...Rf2; 3. Kd7, Rd2 + ; 4. Ke6, Re2 + ; 5. Kd6, Rd2 + ; 6. Ke5, Re2 + ; 7. Re4 and e8 = Q is certain.

If the black Rook does not give check with the 5th move, and Black plays something like this: 5. ...Re1; it would be followed by 6. Rf4, Kg7; 7. Rf8 and e8 = Q. For if 7. ...Rd1 +, the white King advances towards the black Rook until no more checks are possible, e.g. 8. Kc5, Rc1; 9. Kd4, etc.

The edge Pawn does not win.

There are only a few positions where the Rook Pawn wins. Normally the white King remains confined on square a8:

1. Rh1, Rc2; 2. Rh7 +, Kc8; 3. Rh8 +, Kc7; 4. Rb8, Rh2; 5. Rb7 +, Kc8; 6. Rb8 +, Kc7; 7. Rb1, Rh8 + ; 8. Rb8, Rc8! with a draw, i.e. 9. R × c8 forced, K × c8!

How Does One Plan Rook Endings?

Is it the same for the attacker as well as the defender?

Capablanca, a masterly chess technician, once said to Dr. Euwe that he had analysed over a thousand Rook endings in his life. Every tournament player knows that a Rook ending is the most frequent end game. It is essential that one knows some general principles and strategies.

The main task of the Rooks in an end game is to penetrate the ranks of the opposing Pawns, and to try and gain material advantages. The Rook is especially suited to attack the opposing Pawns on the 7th rank as White, or the 2nd rank as Black. Classic are the comments by Richard Réti on the following end game.

"It is extremely instructive, how Capablanca is no longer very interested in the material balance, but thinks only about how to support the passed Pawn."

Capablanca v. Dr. Tartakower
New York 1924

69

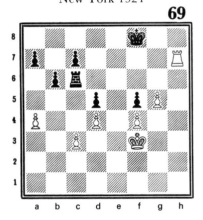

1. Kg3, R × c3 + ; 2. Kh4, Rf3; 3. g6, R × f4 + ; 4. Kg5,

Just as important as the aggressive role of the Rook in such an end game, is the quick approach of the King towards that part of the board where the best chances for the attacker are; that is, where the passed Pawn is.

4. ... Re4; 5. Kf6!

Let us continue quoting Grandmaster Réti: "Not to take the opposing Pawns, but to go past

them so as to gain back-cover from checks by the opposing Rook, is an artifice which one can use frequently."

5. ... Kg8; 6. Rg7 + , Kh8; 7. R × c7, Re8; 8. K × f5, *see* diagram 70.

"White now liquidates material, as Black is obviously quite helpless after this development."

70

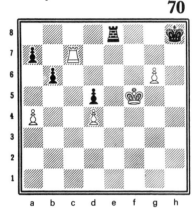

8. ... Re4; 9. Kf6, Rf4 + ; 10. Ke5, Rg4; 11. g7 + , Kg8;

"After a Rook exchange White, of course, would win even more easily."

12. R × a7, Rg1; 13. K × d5,

And Black gave in after another five moves.

Réti concluded: "When one replays such an end game, everything seems to be self-evident, so that one easily forgets the difficulties of such a precise handling of it. Of course *the difficulty is of a psychological nature*: one is so used to evaluating material advantage in chess, as in life generally, that one does not arrive easily at the idea of sacrificing Pawns when so few pieces are on the board."

Speed is the watchword in Rook endings

The former world champion Dr. Euwe, shows in the following example, diagram 71, that speed is the most important principle in Rook endings. Even when in an inferior position it is possible to master the situation by decisive and quick pursuit of one's opportunities. Rook endings are lost if played passively; that is when one only takes defensive precautions. Dr. Euwe wrote in 1943, in a German chess magazine: "One has never won as long as one is not in sole possession of the attack, but equally one has never lost, as long as one can offer some threat. The real objective is victory, that is the queening of one's Pawns, and all other objectives fade into the background. What is the use of one more Pawn when the opponent achieves a Queen earlier? One has to think in a different currency, not in units of material values, but in units of time: *speed, to gain tempo, that is the solution.*"

1. Rc4, R × g2; 2. R × a4, f5;

Black's only plus is the passed Pawn on the f file. It must be his overriding goal to get it moving, and to protect it.

3. R × h4, Kf7; 4. Rh6, f4!; 5. R × c6, f3;

Only one against three is left, but it is a dangerous *one*!

6. Rc4, f2;

van de Hoek v. Dr. Euwe

71

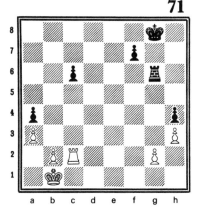

White lost valuable time when he took the Pawn on c6. The black Pawn now forces White to take time consuming defensive measures.

7. Rf4 +, Ke6; 8. Ka2, Ke5; 9. Rf8, Ke4; 10. a4, Ke3;

Black now threatens to win with ... Rg3 followed by ... Rf3. White therefore establishes the draw by move repetition:

11. Re8 +, Kd3; 12. Rd8 +, Ke3; 13. Re8 + a draw.

The active and passive Rook

Each side possesses a passed Pawn, that is ready for queening on the last but one rank. But Black commands the active Rook position—namely, behind the opponent's passed Pawn; while White with a Rook on h8 is in a passive position. If this Rook moves, then the passed Pawn on h7 is lost.

At the moment, however, Black cannot undertake much, for if

Opocensky v. Keres 1939

72

White loses

1. ... Kb1; 2. Rb8 +, Ka1; 3. Rc8, Kb2; 4. Rb8 +, etc. Also if 1. ... Kb1; 2. Rb8 +, Ka1; 3. Rc8, Rh2; 4. R × c2!, R × h7; would be a useless attempt.

Grandmaster Keres won like this:

1. Ka5,

If 1. Kb4?, Black wins straight away because after 1. ... Kb2; the white Rook is no longer in the position to give check on b8.

1. ... Rh4; 2. Ka6, Rh5!; 3. Ka7, Kb2; 4. Rb8 +, Ka2; 5. Rc8, R × h7 +;

White having lost his Pawn and being in check at the same time, can now resign.

Can Three Pawns Win Against Two?

The majority of chess players know that normally Rook end games cannot be won with only one Pawn advantage, if all the

Eisinger v. Schuster
(Baden against Württ. 1948)

73

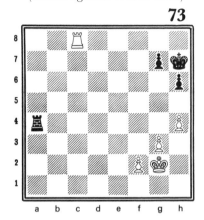

Pawns are on the same side of the board. However, attempts to win such a game are still undertaken, even in World Championships. How interesting that can prove to be, is shown in the following ending—*see* diagram 73.

1. h5, Ra2; 2. g4, Ra3; 3. f3, Ra4; 4. Rd8, Rb4; 5. Kg3, Ra4; 6. Kf2, Rb4; 7. Ke3, Ra4; 8. f4, Rb4; 9. Rd4, Rb5; 10. Ke4, Ra5; 11. Rd5, Ra4 +; 12. Kf5,

Black could not prevent the advance of the King, but should not lose. In a tournament it is a matter of keeping one's nerve. The moment must come when the white King remains under threat of check by the black Rook, or the white Pawns need protection.

12. ... Ra1; 13. Ke6,

If 13. g5, then Black would clear the situation straightaway with 13. ... h × g5; 14. f × g5,

40

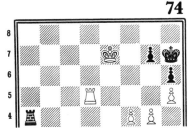

74

Rf1 + ; 15.Ke6, Rh1; 16.g6 + , Kh6; 17.Kf7, Rf1 + ; 18.Kg8, Rf8 + !;—stalemate!

But in this game too, the decision came quickly:

13. ... Ra6 + ; 14.Ke7, Ra4!;
    See diagram 74.

15.g5, Re4 + ;
    And a draw, for 16.Re5, R × f4; 17.g6 + , Kg8; followed by Rf8, and nothing else is possible.

Capablanca once managed to win with four Pawns against three. His opponent, Sir George Thomas, however, committed a small inexactitude, and that was quite sufficient for Capablanca. Why else should he have analysed over a thousand Rook end games?

Two connected passed Pawns on the 6th rank, win against the Rook

Two connected passed Pawns are one of the most powerful weapons in the end game. If these two connected passed Pawns are on the 6th (3rd) rank, not even a Rook can stop them:

1. ... Rg1; 2.f7, Rf1; 3.g7,
    One of the Pawns gets to its goal,

75

Black to move loses
or :

1. ... Re6; 2.f7 (or g7), Rf6; 3.g7, etc.

Routes to Checkmate which One Ought to Know

Two important rules relating to drawn games

Checkmating the King by using two Bishops is not difficult. Even from the most unfavourable position it can be done in 21 moves.

Achieving checkmate with N + B, however, demands a considerable amount of knowledge. From an unfavourable position 35 moves are needed for checkmate. If, however, 50 moves or more are made, then the opponent can claim a draw according to Article 12.4 of the Laws of Chess of *The Fédération Internationale des Echecs.* This paragraph states that the game is drawn "when the player

41

whose turn it is to move proves that at least fifty moves have been played by each side without a capture of a piece and without a Pawn move having been made". Thus the rule not only holds for checkmating with King and Queen against King, but for other situations as well. It can be seen then, that the rule is of considerable practical importance in relation to end games. Note, too, that if a piece has been taken or a Pawn has been moved, then the counting of the 50 moves has to start afresh!

Perpetual check

Diagram 76 shows the position before the 53rd move by White. It started 50 moves of continuous checks by Black.

53. Qa2 + , Kh8; 54. Qb3, Qe4 + ; 55. Kf2, Qf4; 56. Ke2, Qh2 + ; 57. Kd1, Qh1 + ; 58. Kc2, Qg2 + ; 59. Kb1, Qh1 + ; 60. Ka2, Qg2 + ; 61. Ka3, Qa8 + ; 62. Kb4, Qf8 + ; 63. Ka5, Qa8 + ; 64. Kb6, Qb8 + ; 65. Kc6, Qc8 + ; 66. Kd6, Qd8 + ; 67. Ke5, Qf6 + ; 68. Ke4, Qh4 + ; 69. Kd5, Qd8 + ; 70. Kc4, Qh4 + ; 71. Kc5, Qe7 + ; 72. Kc6, Qe8 + ; 73. Kc7, Qe7 + ; 74. Kb8, Qd8 + ; 75. Kb7, Qd7 + ; 76. Ka6, Qc8 + ; 77. Ka5, Qa8 + ;

This position has now appeared for the second time. Previously it was on the board after Black's 63rd move.

If the same position occurs for the third time, then Black can claim a draw. White is therefore on guard, and moves his King carefully back again:

50 consecutive checks

76

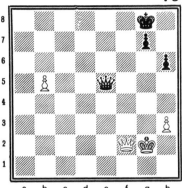

Dr. Lehmann v. Eisinger
German Championship 1957

78. Kb4, Qf8 + ;

A position which appeared on the board after the 62nd move.

79. Kc3, Qf6 + ; 80. Kc2, Qf2 + ; 81. Kb1, Qe1 + ; 82. Kc2, Qe2 + ; 83. Kc3, Qe5 + ; 84. Kd2, Qf4 + ; 85. Ke1, Qe4 + ; 86. Kd1, Qd4 + ; 87. Kc1, Qf4 + ; 88. Kb1, Qf1 + ; 89. Kb2, Qe2 + ; 90. Ka3, Qe7 + ; 91. Qb4, Qa7 + ;

Note that similar positions could now be repeated without risk of a draw by repetition, since none of them would be completely the same again because of the changed position of the white Queen (from b3 to b4)!

92. Kb3, Qe3 + ; 93. Qc3, Qe6 + ; 94. Kb4, Qe7 + ; 95. Qc5, Qe1 + ; 96. Kc4, Qf1 + ; 97. Kd5, Qf3 + ; 98. Ke6, Qf6 + ;

Black is careful not to take the Pawn on h3, because counting of the 50 moves would then start afresh. He wants to acquit himself of 50 moves without taking a piece or moving a Pawn! 99. Kd7, Qf7 + ; 100. Kc8, Qe8 + ; 101. Kb7, Qd7 + ; 102. Kb8, Qe8 + ; 103. Qc8, a draw!

Just when Black is on the verge of losing by compulsory exchange of Queens, with the white passed Pawn free to reach b8 easily—the limit of 50 moves has been reached.

Black appealed to the chairman of the tournament, who on demand had to declare the game a draw according to Article 12. Black could have moved 103. ... Kg8; without risk of loss, because White is not allowed to continue the game. Move 103. Qc8 was already the 51st move without the loss of a piece or the move of a Pawn.

By the way, the 50 moves by Black did not need to involve giving check every time, as is illustrated here.

A second danger of a draw, in a difficult situation, consists of the recurrence of a position three times. According to Article 12.3 a game ends in a draw: "At the request of one of the players, when the same position appears three times, and each time the same player has had the move. The position is considered the same if pieces of the same kind and colour occupy the same squares, and if the possible moves of all the pieces are the same."

Chessplayers frequently speak of "repeat-moves" as reason for a draw. However, it is more correct to speak of "position-repetition", because only the triple repetition of the same position entitles a player to demand a draw. Thus perpetual check can take place in three moves, namely when White and Black must play the same moves three times.

But it is not necessary that the same position occurs three times in succession! It is sufficient for example, when the same position occurs in the 36th, 44th, and maybe the 70th moves.

We should notice, however, that it is essential to write down each move if a draw is to be claimed under the 50 move rule, or because of the triple repetition of position. The player must be able to produce evidence that 50 moves have taken place without the taking of a piece or the move of a Pawn; or that the same position will occur three times (for the player must claim a draw before the decisive 3rd move takes place, but must not carry it out!). In practice, this means that in a lightning tournament where moves are not written down, and in private unrecorded games, the right to demand a draw cannot be claimed.

We will now consider positions involving Q v. R, Q v. R + P, N + B v. K, R + B v. R.

Queen Against Rook

Queen against Rook certainly wins, even if the path to victory is

77

not an easy one.

The King must be forced to the edge, which will compel the Rook to move away from its own King. Subsequently it will be easy to take the Rook when giving check with the Queen. The side with the Queen, however, has to watch out not to create a stalemate position. From diagram 77:

1. Ke3,   Rf5;   2. Qc3 +,   Kd5;
3. Qd4 +, Ke6; 4. Ke4, Rf6;

Journeys by the Rook lead to its loss, for example 4. ... Ra5; 5. Qb6 +, or 4. ... Rf1; 5. Qc4 +.

5. Qd5 +,   Ke7;   6. Ke5,   Rf7;
7. Qd6 +, Ke8;

See diagram 78.

78

Watch out for stalemate!

Not 8. Ke6?, Rf6 + !; 9. K × f6, stalemate. Therefore:

8. Qb8 +,   Kd7;   9. Qb7 +,   Ke8;
10. Qc8 +,   Ke7;   11. Qc4—a
waiting move.

If the Rook moves away, the Queen will take it, e.g.   11. ... Rf2?;   12. Qc5, or 11. ... Rf3;   12. Qc7 +,   Kf8; 13. Qc8 +,   Kg7;   14. Qg4 +. Equally hopeless would be 11. ... Rh7;   or   11. ... Rf6; 12. Qc7 +, etc.

11. ... Kf8; 12. Ke6, Kg8; 13. Qd5, Rg7;   14. Kf6 +,   Kh8;   15. Qe5, Kh7;

Moves by the Rook would mean its loss.

16. Qe8 !

A waiting move, which puts Black into *zugzwang*. 16. ... Kh6 is followed by 17. Qf8, which pins the Rook and wins it. If, however, the Rook moves, it becomes the victim of the Queen. For example:

16. ... Rg1;

And now follow the "zig-zag" checks.

17. Qd7 +, Kh8; 18. Qc8 +, Kh7;
If 18. ... Rg8; 19. Qh3 + ;

19. Qc7 + !, Kg8;
If 19. ... Kh7; 20. Qh2 +,

20. Qb8 + followed by Qa7 + captures the Rook on g1, with mate to follow on one move.

Note that after the capture of the Rook, the counting of the 50 moves would have to begin afresh, because one of the pieces has been taken. Moreover, checkmate by the Queen against the King can be achieved in a minimum of 10 moves from the most unfavourable position.

Queen against Rook and Pawn

In certain positions, as in the two diagrams 79 and 80, it is not possible for the Queen to win against Rook and Pawn. In diagram 79 the black Rook has firm hold on the squares c6 and e6, and in diagram 80, f6 and h6. The attacking King cannot advance.

The Queen, however, can achieve victory if the defender's Pawn is no longer on the 2nd (7th) rank, apart from some exceptions.

Drawn position

Checkmate with Knight and Bishop

The W-system of the Knight

Knight and Bishop constitute the smallest force with which to achieve checkmate against a lone King. With two Knights the checkmate is possible only with the help of the opponent. If, however, the opponent is still in possession of Pawns, two Knights may achieve checkmate provided that the Pawns can be blocked in in time.

Many a player in a tournament did not achieve checkmate within the 50 move limit with N + B, which seems to indicate the usefulness of some knowledge of this relatively simple strategy. The following position may suffice as an exercise:

White Ka1 Ba8 Nh8
Black Ke5

Checkmate can only be achieved with the defending King on a corner square which is the same colour as those on which the Bishop moves.

To know this is especially important for the defending side, because as long as the King sits in the wrong corner, checkmate is impossible.

It should take from 14–16 moves to get from our starting position to that in diagram 81.

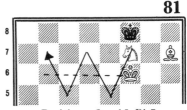

Position after 15.Bh7

Checkmate can be achieved in a further 17 moves. From our starting position the moves are as follows:

1. Kb2, Kf6; 2. Be4, Ke5; 3. Bd3, Kf6; 4. Kc3, Ke5; 5. Ng6+, Kf6;

The black King remains in its correct corner as long as possible, namely in the opposite coloured square to that of the Bishop.

6. Be4, Ke6; 7. Kd4, Kf6; 8. Kd5, Kg5; 9. Ke5, Kh6;

Or 9. ... Kg4; 10. Kf6, Kg3; 11. Kf5, Kf2; 12. Kf4, etc.

10. Kf6, Kh5; 11. Bf3+, Kh6; 12. Ne5, Kh7; 13. Nf7, Kg8; 14. Be4, Kf8; 15. Bh7!

This takes us to the position in diagram 81.

Now begins the important stage of driving the King into the corner a8. The white pieces have the following systematic tasks: The Knight follows the route of the W-system f7—e5—d7—c5—b7; the white King moves without deviations along the 6th rank towards square b6; the Bishop prevents an escape of the black King beyond square c6, by positioning himself along the diagonal f1—a6, and on the next move along diagonal h1—a8.

The sequence is now:

15. ... Ke8; 16. Ne5, Kd8; 17. Ke6, Kc7;

This is a critical moment, because the defending King threatens to escape via b6 or c6. Whoever does not know the next three moves will find himself chasing the King endlessly around the board.

18. Nd7!, Kc6; 19. Bd3!, Kc7; 20. Be4!,

All dangers are over. The

82

King is driven once more on to the back rank.

20. ... Kd8; 21. Kd6, Ke8; 22. Bd5, *see* diagram 82.

22. ... Kd8; 23. Bf7, Kc8; 24. Nc5, Kd8; 25. Nb7+, Kc8; 26. Kc6, Kb8; 27. Kb6, Kc8; 28. Be6+, Kb8; 29. Nc5, Ka8;

Now the typical finish:

30. Bh3,

Or any other square on diagonal h3–c8 except c8.

30. ... Kb8; 31. Na6+, Ka8; 32. Bg2 ‡

If the Bishop were operating on black squares, then the mate could take place on the corresponding black square h8 as follows: the Knight would move in the well-known W-formation of c7—d5—e7—f5—g7; the Bishop would cut off the square b8 with Ba7, then at the critical moment take up position along the diagonal c1–h6 (that is on e3), arriving at the next move along the mid-diagonal h1–a8 (square d4).

Checkmate with Rook and Bishop Against Rook

It is not possible to achieve checkmate with Rook and Bishop in every case; nine out of ten positions will lead to a draw. The defence demands a great deal of vigilance, as does success in those exceptional positions that have winning possibilities.

Using diagram 83, we can follow the ingenious and fundamental winning line by Philidor, which the French Master analysed in 1749.

Notice first of all, that the defending Rook has taken up his

Winning strategy by Philidor

83

position on White's 7th rank, in order to fend off the opposing King. Victory is possible only if White is to move first.

If 1.Bc6, the threat of 2.Rf8+ with mate to follow, is thwarted by 1....Rd7+!; 2.B×d7, a draw. If Black had a Pawn, say on a5, the game would have been lost for him because of this attack.

In the original position, however, White has to play as follows:

1.Rf8+, Re8; 2.Rf7, Re2!;

   2....Rh8 is a bad move, because 3.Ra7, Rh6+; 4.Be6 decides the issue straightaway.

   It can be seen that White has to force the Rook to e3 in order to win.

3.Rg7, Re1;

   If 3....Re3; the continuation would be the same, except that after 4....Rc3; White could play Rd7+ at the 5th move rather than at the 8th—*see* page 47.

   3....Re8; is a bad move because of 4.Ra7.

4.Rb7, Rc1;

   If 4....Kc8; then 5.Ra7, Rb1; 6.Rf7, Kb8; 7.Rf8+, Ka7; 8.Ra8+, Kb6; 9.Rb8+, and wins the Rook.

   Or 6....Rb6+; 7.Bc6, Kb8; 8.Rf8+, Ka8; 9.Ra8≠. This variation plays an important part.

5.Bb3, Rc3; *see* diagram 84.

   This move by the Rook guarantees the longest defence. After 5....Kc8; there would follow 6.Rb4, (threatening Be6+) 6....Kd8; 7.Rf4, Re1; 8.Ba4, Kc8; 9.Bc6, Rd1+; 10.Bd5, Kb8; 11.Ra4 and Ra8≠ follows.

6.Be6, Rd3+; 7.Bd5, Rc3;

   Or 7....Kc8; 8.Ra7 and the black Rook cannot move on to the b file.

8.Rd7+, Kc8;

   Notice that Black cannot play 8....Ke8, because 9.Rg7 with Rg8 to follow, wins; because the

84

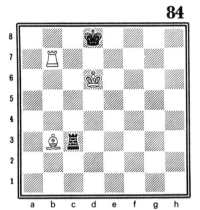

black Rook has no time to interpose at f8.

9. Rf7, Kb8; 10. Rb7+, Kc8; 11. Rb4, Kd8;

If 11. ... Rd3; in order to pin the Bishop, 12. Ra4 wins at once.

12. Bc4, Kc8; 13. Be6+, Kd8 forced; 14. Rb8+, Rc8 forced; 15. R × c8 ‡

Winning strategy by Lolli

85

In this relatively easy strategy, the attacking Rook occupied seven files a–g. It is clear that such freedom occurs only when the Kings stand on central files d or e. More advantageous for the defence is an original position with the Kings on either of the Bishop files c or f. Yet the Italian Lolli demonstrated in 1763 that even then a victory is easily possible.

From diagram 85, White wins, as follows:

1. Re8+, Rd8; 2. Re7,
   And now:

Variation A

2. ... Rg8;
   The alternative 2. ... Rh8; loses quickly because of 3. Bd6, Kd8; 4. Ra7, Ke8; 5. Ra8+ and the Rook on h8 is lost; while the Rook on g8 is protected by Kf7.

3. Ra7, Kb8;
   Not 3. ... Rg6+; 4. Bd6 wins the Rook or checkmate.

4. Rb7+, Ka8;
   4. ... Kc8; 5. Bd6, etc.

5. Bd6, Rc8+;
   See diagram 86.

86

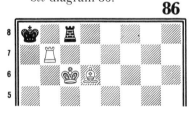

If 5. ... Rg1; then 6. Rb8+, Ka7; 7. Rh8, threatening Bc5+, etc. Or if 7. ... Rg6; 8. Rh1 and Ra1 ‡.

But if 5. ... Rg7 attempting to

achieve a draw, then 6. Rb8 + , Ka7; 7. Rb1, Ka8; 8. Re1 as in the main continuation that follows.

Even worse would be 5. ... Rh8; or 5. ... Re8 or d8; because 6. Rb1 follows.

6. Bc7, Rh8; 7. Rb1, Rh6 + ; 8. Bd6, Rh7; 9. Re1, Rg7; 10. Re8 + , Ka7; 11. Bc5 + and mates in two moves

Now reverting back to the position in diagram 85, consider an alternative variation from Black's second move:

Variation B
2. ... Rd2; 3. Rf7, Rd8;

This defence is omitted completely in the example by Philidor with the King on d6 and Bishop on d5. If Black moves instead 3. ... Rd1; it would be followed by —analogous with the position by Philidor—4. Ra7, but with the difference that after 4. ... Rb1; 5. Ba3, Kb8. Now not 6. Ra4 but 6. Re7!, 6. ... Ka8; 7. Re4, Rb7;

8. Re5, a waiting move which compels Black to abandon his good defensive position. *See* diagram 87. Lolli indicates that White achieves checkmate in a further four moves:

8. ... Ka7; or 8. ... Rb1; 9. Ra5 + , Kb8; 10. Bd6 + , etc. Or 8. ... Kb8; 9. Re8 + followed by 10. Bc5 + , etc. Note that after 3. ... Rd1; 4. Ra7, if 4. ... Kb8; instead of 4. ... Rb1; the following moves would lead to a quicker decision: 5. Ra4, Rc1; 6. Re4.

Similarly, in comparison with Philidor's position, after 2. ... Rd2; 3. Rf7, Rd1; 4. Ra7, Rb1; 5. Ba3, Rb3; Black loses more quickly because the defending King has no further escape route on the left side after 6. Bd6, Rc3 + ; 7. Bc5, Rb3; 8. Rc7 + , Kb8; 9. Rf7.

To return to the main problem:
4. Be7, Rg8;
See diagram 88.

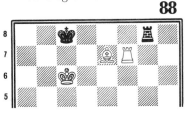

After 4. ... Re8; White could play 5. Rf5! or 5. Bd6!
5. Rf5, Kb8;
Or 5. ... Rg6 + ; 6. Bd6, Rg8; 7. Ra5, etc.
6. Bd6 + , Kc8; 7. Ra5 or b5,
And mate follows on the 8th rank.

A win overlooked

The Dutch Master Böhm arrived at this winning position after 164! moves during the IBM Tournament in Amsterdam. White looked at the board for 40 minutes and finally played 165.Rg2? Of course, the Argentinian Master replied 165 ... Re3; and was saved: 166.Ra2, Ra3. White had to accept a draw after another few moves because of the 50 move rule, for it was not possible to mate Black within the required number of moves.

Yet victory could have been achieved easily from the position in diagram 89 with:

165.Rg4+!, Ka3; 166.Rg2 followed by Ra2 ≠.

If 165....Ka5; then checkmate on the a file with either Rg2 or Rg8.

Böhm v. Debarnot
IBM Tournament 1974

Rook and Knight against Rook: A Draw

Rook and Knight against Rook usually ends in a draw. A win for the stronger side is possible, only if the opposing King has already been forced to the side.

See diagram 90. With White to move, there are no difficulties, for checkmate is brought about by:

1.Ra8+, Kh7; 2.Ng5+, Kh6; 3.Rh8≠.

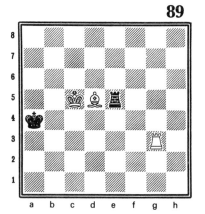

90

White forces checkmate

With Black to move:

1....Rb6+; 2.Kf7, Rb7+; 3.Kg6, Rb6+; 4.Nf6 wins, or:
4.Kg6, Rg7+; 5.Kf6, Rg1; 6.Ng5, Rf1+; 7.Kg6, Rf8; 8.Nf7+, Kg8; 9.Nh6+, Kh8; 10.Rh2,

And either Black must allow 11.Nf7+, etc. or 10....Rg8+; 11.N×g8, K×g8; 12.Rf2, Kh8; 13.Rf8≠.

89

The situation is in no way better for Black if he plays:

1. ... Rf1 + ; 2. Kg6, Rg1 + ; 3. Ng5,
And there is no remedy against Ra8 + .

There is also:

1. ... Rb8; 2. Kf7, Rb7 + ; 3. Kg6, Rg7 + ; 4. Kf6, etc. as above.

Rook against Bishop: a draw

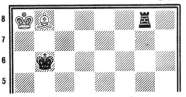

91

Black cannot win

The defender must aim to reach a corner square with his King, which is not the same colour as that on which the Bishop moves. All attempts by White lead to a draw. *See* diagram 91:

1. ... Rg7; 2. Bh2, Ra7 + ; 3. Kb8, Rh7; 4. Bg1 + , Ka6; 5. Bd4, Rd7; 6. Bf2, Rf7; 7. Be3, a draw.

Rook against Knight: a draw

Only in exceptional cases can the Rook win against a Knight. In this position in diagram 92, the

92

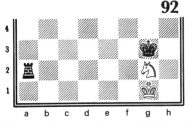

White obtains a draw with 1. Ne1

Knight achieves a draw, although White had already been confined to the side.

1. Ne1, Ra1; 2. Kf1, Ra2; 3. Kg1, Rf2; 4. Nd3, Rd2; 5. Ne1, Ra2; 6. Kf1, a draw.

Knight against Pawn: the Knight can stop an edge Pawn

93

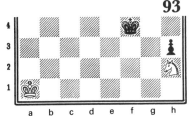

Black to move: a draw

1. ... Kg3; 2. Nf1 + , Kg2; 3. Ne3 + , Kf3; 4. Nf1, Kf2; 5. Nh2, Kg2; 6. Ng4, Kg3;

Has the Knight now been neutralized? No, threat of a fork saves the situation!

7. Ne3! h2; 8. Nf1 + , a draw.

In cases of a Pawn on a file other than an edge file, it is even more difficult for the opposing King to get near the Knight.

Bishop and Pawn against Bishop

A Bishop is forced away

First of all White must force the opposing Bishop off the long diagonal:

1. Bd7, Bf3; 2. Bc8, Bd5; 3. Bb7, Bc4; 4. Be4, Ba6; 5. Bd3!

White has still not won, but Black has been manoeuvred into *zugzwang*.

5. ... Bc8; 6. Be2,

94

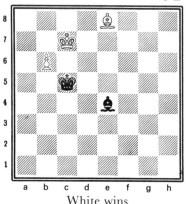

White wins

Black must now either move his Bishop away from the guard on b7, or move the King away from the Pawn, say 6....Kd5. In either case White plays 7.b7, and wins.

An end game brilliancy

An artful battle with the same number of Bishops and passed Pawns provides those who re-play the moves with useful knowledge and strategies for end games.

White possesses a dangerous passed Pawn on a6, which is carefully watched by the black King. Black obtains another passed Pawn after his next move. But it becomes quite clear in what follows, that White's well advanced passed Pawn is much more dangerous than Black's. From diagram 95:

56. B × e5, B × h4; 57. f4, Bg3;

Black intends to get his passed Pawn moving with h4–h3–h2.

58. Bb8!, Bf2;

Black has to abandon his

Larsen v. Quinteros, Grandmaster Tournament, Las Palmas 1974

95

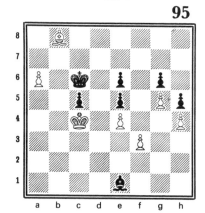

Position after the 55th move

plan. Observe: If 58....h4?; 59. a7!, Kb7; 60. f5, B × b8; 61. a × b8 +, K × b8; 62. f × g6, and a new Queen arrives first on g8, giving check.

59. f5, e × f5; 60. e × f5, g × f5; 61. g6, Bd4; 62. Bd6!!

96

Position after 62. Bd6!!

This artful move demonstrates quite clearly the danger of the Pawn on a6. The black King must not take the Bishop, otherwise this Pawn is through to a8.

62. ... h4; 63. B × c5!,

Here too, the Bishop cannot be taken, if the g Pawn is to be prevented from queening. The same would also have happened in response to 62. ... Kb6; 63. B × c5 + and a quick end.

63. ... Bg7; 64. Bg1, h3; 65. Kd3, Bh6; 66. Ke2, h2; 67. B × h2, Kb6; 68. Kd3, K × a6; 69. Kc4, Kb6;

Taking the Pawn at a6 lost the black King valuable time and space. The white King arrives at f7 first.

70. Kd5, Kb5; 71. Bf4!, Bg7; 72. Be5, Bh6; 73. Ke6, Kc6; 74. Kf7,

Black gives in after.

74. ... Kd7; 75. Bf4!

Black's Bishop has no room left to cover the advance of the white Pawn to g7. It is forced away.

Qualitative Imbalance

The surplus value of the Rook as measured against the Bishop, or of the Rook against the Knight is a significant qualitative difference. If one exchanges a Bishop or a Knight for a Rook, one gains a material advantage, and speaks of *winning the exchange*. Of course it is possible to sacrifice this exchange advantage in order to gain positional advantages, especially in the

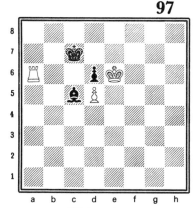

97

White wins

middle game and during an attack. In the end game, however, the greater value through having won the exchange is, as a rule, of decisive importance when there are still Pawns left on the board.

In diagram 97, victory by White is achieved simply, when the Rook takes the Pawn on d6 at the right moment, and then proceeds to win the pawn ending.

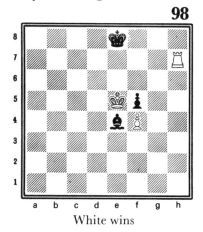

98

White wins

Thus:

1. Rc6+, Kd8; 2. R×d6+, B×d6; 3. K×d6 and wins.

In diagram 98, White cannot use the same strategy, sacrificing the Rook on f5, because the black King could then go into opposition on f7. First of all the black King must be forced away.

1. Kf6, Bd3; 2. Re7+, Kd8;

Objective achieved, for if 2. ... Kf8; 3. Rd7 wins the Bishop.

3. Re5,   Be4;   4. R×f5,   B×f5; 5. K×f5,

And wins, for the black King can no longer gain the opposition.

How Many Queens are Allowed?

A lesson about queening.

Vidmar v. Yates Hastings 1925

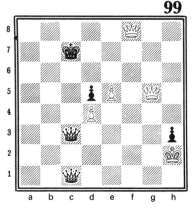

99

Those inexperienced in chess will look at the position in diagram 99 in amazement, if not indignation. Is it at all permissible to obtain a second Queen when the first Queen is still on the board?

In this case there are even four Queens on the board! It cannot be repeated too often, that a player is free to exchange Pawns on the last rank for any piece of his choice, of the same colour; except of course a King. It does not matter that the original Queen is still on the board; a player could even then obtain a second, third, fourth or more Queens.

Equally, three or more Knights or Bishops are permissible. There are no limitations as Article 6(c) of the rules indicates: "On reaching the end of a file a Pawn must be immediately exchanged, as part of the same move, for a Queen, a Rook, a Bishop or a Knight at the player's choice and without taking into account the other pieces still remaining on the chess board. This exchanging of a Pawn is called *promotion*. The promoted piece must be of the same colour as the Pawn and its action is immediate."

Theoretically then, it is possible for one side to have nine Queens on the board, one from the original position and eight obtained by queening.

See diagram 99. White to move achieves checkmate in four moves: 1. Qg5—d8+, Kc6; 2. Qf8—e8+, Kb7; 3. Qb5+, Ka7; 4. Qd8—b8‡

In some cases it is wise not to promote a Pawn for the most powerful piece, but for a weaker one. Here is a simple example of such *under-promotion*.

Promotion to a Rook

100

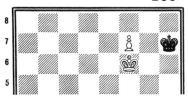

A too hasty move would be 1.f8 = Q?, a draw by stalemate. Correct is to under-promote, that is:

1.f8 = R!

Now the black King is able to move to h6, whereupon Rh8 gives checkmate.

Promoting to a Knight

101

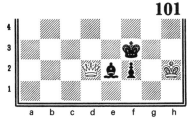

It would be a disappointing ending for Black if he played 1....f1 = Q? White would of course answer with 2.Qf4 +, Kf4; and obtain a draw, again by stalemate.

A more modest promotion is much more effective:

1....f1 = N + !

Followed by N × e7, after which Knight and Bishop achieve checkmate.

Underpromoting to a Bishop or Rook is frequently found in chess problems and studies.

The "Wrong" Bishop

White to move played 1.Kg1! Is not such a move by White almost unbelievable? Indeed is it not a mistake? Knowledge of the "wrong" Bishop solves the puzzle of the unbelievable move by the white King.

An unbelievable move?

102

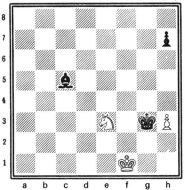

Rellstab v. Machate Essen 1948

The fact is, that Black can no longer win once the white King reaches the corner square h1! Although Black then possesses a Bishop and a Rook's Pawn, against the lonely white King, the position is a draw. Black owns a Bishop of the "wrong" colour! The defending King cannot be shifted from square h1 by the black-squared Bishop or the Rook's Pawn. He can only be stalemated:

1.Kg1!, B × e3 + ; 2.Kh1, Kf2;
　　2....K × h3? a draw.

In this particular match during the German Championships, Machate (Black) moved 2....Be3—

55

e4 + !?; an illegal move, just for fun, and with a smile confirmed the unavoidable draw.

We know that Bishops and Rook Pawns are useless if *the Bishop is not operating on squares of the same colour as the queening square*! The defending King has simply to go all out to get to the queening square.

The Masters of the 17th century knew this, for Greco demonstrated this well-known end game position in 1621:

White: Ke5 Rh2 Bf1
Black Kb8 Rc7 Bc6 Pa7 b7

Black may well be hopeful of winning with two connected passed Pawns, and Bishops of the same colour squares, but:

1. Rh8+, Rc8; 2. R × c8+, K × c8; 3. Ba6!!

At first sight, again a quite unbelievable move. But the sacrifice of the Bishop creates the most promising position for White. Black is quite helpless. It does not matter whether Black takes the Bishop by 3.…b × a6; or whether he ignores the offered sacrifice. In either event Black will be left with one or two Pawns on the Rook's file with a *Bishop of the wrong colour*! Black cannot prevent White from reaching the corner square a1. Thus after 4. Kd4, a draw!

What ex-World Champion Botvinnik "saw" via the telephone

Robert Fisher began his triumphant road to the World Cham-

R. Fisher v. M. Taimanov
Candidate Tournament 1971

103

pionship with the candidate games in Vancouver 1971. His first opponent was Grandmaster Taimanov, U.S.S.R., who was beaten 6:0. During the second game of this tournament, the above position in diagram 103 was arrived at, and the game was won by White as follows:

1.… Ke4?; 2. Bc8, Kf4; 3. h4, Nf3; 4. h5, Ng5; 5. Bf5, Nf3; 6. h6, Ng5; 7. Kg6, Nf3; 8. h7, Ne5 +; 9. Kf6,

Black resigned and all the world was satisfied. Not so ex-World Champion Dr. Botvinnik, to whom the position in diagram 103 had been sent by telephone, that is *before* 1.… Ke4.

Without a board Botvinnik saw at once that Taimanov, with Black, could have achieved a draw, if only he had remembered the rule of the "wrong" Bishop!

Black could have achieved it in the following way:

1. ... Nd3! 2. h4, Nf4; 3. Kf5, Kd6!!

Black abandons the Knight in order to get to the square that will save him—h8. After 4. K × f4, Ke7. Once again Bishop and Pawn cannot win, because the Bishop is of the wrong colour! If White does not take the Knight, he will still not get any further with his Pawn: 4. Kf6, Nd5+; 5. Kg5, Nf4! a draw.

The strength and weakness of the Knight

104 **105**

Black to move wins

White to move, a draw!

In diagram 104, by moving:

1. ... Kc7;

Black achieves checkmate with his Knight. *Zugzwang* achieves the miracle.

2. Ka8, Nc8; 3. a7, Nb6‡

In diagram 105 we experience something quite unbelievable— Knight and Pawn cannot win against the King! The black King

does not give up the confinement of the white King:

1. Ne6+, Kf7; 2. Kg7, Kf8; 3. Ne8, Kf7! 4. Nd6+, Kf8;

Even if the Knight moves around the whole board, he cannot gain a tempo. For example he cannot manoeuvre his Knight on to h6 with the black King on f1 to move—a winning position. Initially he is on the wrong coloured square.

The "wrong" Knight

Stein v. Dorfmann (SU 1973)

106

White achieves a draw

We have just made the acquaintance of the "wrong" Knight, which like the "wrong" Bishop can be on the wrong coloured square.

Such an end game position is not only of theoretical importance; it occurs frequently, and is a matter of recognizing the opportunity.

This is what happened following the position in diagram 106:

1. Bf6, Nd3;

57

Black threatens to cut off the Bishop from the square a1 with Nb2, which therefore dictates the following moves:

2. Ba1, Nb2; 3. Ke1, Kb1; 4. Kd2!, K × a1;

The draw is now quite obvious. Alternatively 4. ... Nc4+; 5. Kd1, K × a1; 6. Kc2! Beware not to move on to a square of the opposite colour to that on which the Knight stands, e.g. 6. Kc1??, Na3 or e3; and Black wins as his King can now escape from its confinement.

The game concluded:

5. Kc1!, Nc4; 6. Kc2, a draw!

Pawn Majority in the End Game

We speak of a pawn majority when one side possesses 4 against 3, 3 against 2 or 2 against 1 Pawn on one wing. The side with the additional Pawn will attempt to obtain a passed Pawn on that wing, and to advance it on to the last rank. Not until Wilhelm Steinitz (1836–1900) were such positional laws formulated.

The chances for either side must be judged to be equal. In the end White will obtain a passed Pawn on the Queen's wing, and Black one on the King's wing. The game ought therefore to end in a draw.

At the beginning of a game, Black obtains a pawn majority on the Queen's wing after 1. d4, Nf6; 2. c4, e6; 3. Nc3, d5; 4. Nf3, c5; 5. c × d5, N × d5; 6. e4, N × c3;

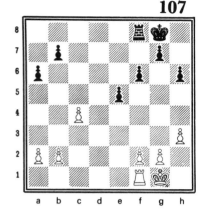

107

White majority on the Queen's wing Black majority on the King's wing

7. b × c3, c × d4; 8. c × d4 (a7 and b7 against a2).

It is a different matter, however, when a pawn majority is devalued by a doubled Pawn. This happens frequently following a general exchange, in the Ruy Lopez opening: 1. e4, e5; 2. Nf3, Nc6; 3. Bb5, a6; 4. B × c6, d × c6; 5. d4, e × d4; 6. Q × d4, Q × d4; 7. N × d4, and after further exchange of pieces during the next few moves, the pawn structure looks like that shown in diagram 108.

True, each side has seven Pawns, but the doubled Pawns on the c file constitute a serious disadvantage in a pure pawn ending. White creates a passed Pawn on the King's wing, with the help of his King; while Black cannot achieve the same on the Queen's wing.

108

White wins automatically

For example, after ...b6—b5 White does not capture on b5, but leaves the pawn position as it is. The uselessness of the doubled pawn position becomes quite obvious if Black exchanges by ...b5 × c4; b3 × c4. The Pawns on c7 and c5 have no more value than the one white Pawn on c4.

The way Black can achieve an active game, was demonstrated in the 16th game of the Fisher–Spassky World Championship series 1972: 1.e4, e5; 2.Nf3, Nc6; 3.Bb5, a6; 4.B × c6, d × c6; 5.0–0, f6; 6.d4, Bg4; 7.d × e5, Q × d1; 8.R × d1, f × e5; 9.Rd3, Bd6; 10.Nbd2, Nf6; 11.Nc4, N × e4; 12.Nc × e5, B × f3; 13.N × f3, 0–0; 14.Be3, b5!

Winning with a pawn majority

End games like the one in diagram 109 happen daily. Once Black has allowed himself to be pushed on to the defensive, as in

Dr. Lasker v. Dr. Tarrasch, 1908

109

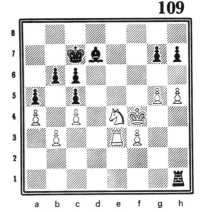

White wins

this case, it is no longer possible to stop victory by the white pawn majority on the King's wing. Black can achieve nothing with his Pawns on the Queen's wing, because White does not react to the advance ...b6—b5.

This ending from the World Championship of 1908 between the two Germans, Lasker and Tarrasch, may serve as an example of how to win:

1.Ng3, Rh4+; 2.Ke5, Rh3; 3.f4, Kd8; 4.f5, Rh4; 5.f6, g × f6+; 6.K × f6, Be8; 7.Nf5!

At this stage a combinational decision is possible; if the Rook captures on h5, then 8.R × e8+, K × e8; 9.Ng7+, capturing the Rook.

7....Rf4; 8.g6, h × g6; 9.h × g6, Rg4; 10.R × e8+,

Also 10.Rg3 leads to a win.

10....K × e8; 11.g7, Kd7; 12.Nh4,

59

R × g7; 13. Kg7, Ke6; 14. Nf3 (or g6), Kf5; 15. Kf7, Ke4; 16. Ke6, Kd3;

If the black King loiters to take the Knight, it will need even more time to get on to the Queen's wing.

17. Kd6, Kc3; 18. K × c6, K × b3; 19. Kb5!

Black resigned

Good against bad Bishop

It is known that two Bishops are stronger than two Knights in an end game. Also Bishop and Knight are slightly stronger than two Knights. However, this is only true in open positions where the Bishops have operational possibilities against the Pawns on both wings. But those are rather refined end game theories, which usually are applied only at Master level.

There is, however, one end game theme which every player ought to know, for it occurs frequently: that is, the good Bishop against the bad Bishop! A pre-condition is that both Bishops are operating on the same colour squares, and that, if possible, relatively fixed pawn structures are in existence on both wings.

See the example in diagram 110.

Black is in possession of the bad Bishop because it is on the same coloured square as his tied Pawns a6/b5 on the Queen's wing. This limits Black's freedom of movement to such an extent that he is forced into *zugzwang*. Black will either lose one of his Pawns directly, or he

Pytel v. Hodjarova
Hungary 1970

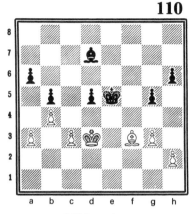

110

White wins

must allow the white King to advance.

1. Bh5!, Bf5 + ; 2. Ke3, Bd7; 3. h4, g4; 4. Bg6, Kf6; 5. Bc2, Ke5; 6. Bd3, Be8; 7. Be2, Bd7;

This is a battle of speed, about turning the flank by a3—a4.

8. Bd1!, Be6; 9. a4, Bd7; 10. a × b5, a × b5; 11. Be2, h5;

Black does not want to be encumbered with covering the Pawn on g4 all the time, but this results in the weakness of h5.

12. Bf1, Bc6; 13. Bd3, Be8; 14. Bc2, Bf7; 15. Bh7, Be8; 16. Bd3, Ke6;

White has obtained his first goal: the King advances and very soon one of the weaklings b5, d5 or h5 will fall.

17. Kd4, Kd6; 18. Bf5, Bf7; 19. Bh7, Be8; 20. Bg8,

The *zugzwang* is complete. Black would lose first one Pawn

and then the others; he therefore resigned.

The Power of the Passed Pawn

Well advanced, passed Pawns

Capablanca v. Villegas
Buenos Aires 1914

111

White to move wins

frequently enable surprising sacrificial decisions. Here are two famous combinational exchanges relating to this theme:

Many a chess player would take quite a time to win with White. Capablanca, who later became World Champion, demonstrates the classical winning moves:

1. Qe5+, f6; 2. Q×d6!, Q×d6; 3. c7,

And Black resigned as the threat of c8 = Q gives White a whole Rook advantage.

The Women's World Champion, Miss Vera Menchik was not able to win a single match against the chess giants Botvinnik, Lasker, Flohr, etc., during the Grandmaster Tournament in Moscow 1935. But

Stahlberg v. Vera Menchik
Grandmaster Tournament,
Moscow 1935

112

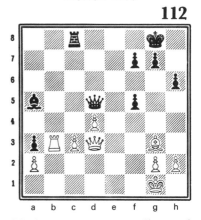

Black to move ... an audience of 4,000 kept their fingers crossed for Vera Menchik!

now the 4,000 people in the tournament hall were crossing their fingers for her, because the Swedish Grandmaster G. Stahlberg had just made a terrible mistake. His last move was 34. Qc2—d3, and no sooner had he let go of the Queen when he noticed his misfortune. As cool as ever, he got up from his chair, walked about and thought to himself: "That's very unpleasant; I will now be the only one who loses his match against a woman."

But what the audience saw, or whispered to each other, the English World Champion did not see in the heat of the battle. She could have won brilliantly by sacrificing her Queen:

34. ... Q × b3! 35. a × b3, a2;

The progress of the Pawn, which has suddenly been made into a passed Pawn, can no longer be stopped.

36. Qd1, B × c3;

Followed by a1 = Q and Black would have won a Rook.

During her chess career, Miss Menchik beat many a Grandmaster, among them the World Champion Dr. Euwe. Miss Menchik died in London in 1944, the victim of a German air-raid.

Queen Endings

End games with Queens and Pawns demand a lot of patience and experience. The danger of perpetual check is often a barrier to victory, or a salvation for the defence.

Here are some practical examples:

White's positional advantage in diagram 113 is based on the following two features: (i) the white Queen has taken up a troublesome position within the Black camp at c6; Black cannot afford to take the Queen because the resultant passed Pawn would then move on to c8 to become a Queen: (ii) the other disadvantage for Black consists in the weakness of the white squares e6/f5/g6/h5. Using these squares, the white King threatens to advance so as to combine with its Queen for the attack.

Hecht v. Villeneuve
France 1971

113

White to move

If 4. ... Qf2; then 5. Kf5!, Q × g2; 6. Qc8 +, Kf7; 7. Qd7 +, 1. h5!, Kf8; 2. Qa8 +, Kf7; 3. Qb7 +, Kf8; 4. Kg4!, Kg8; 8. Qe8 +, Kh7; 9. Ke6, Q × f3; 10. Qg6 +, Kg8; 11. K × d6 and wins.

5. Kf5, Kh7; 6. Ke6, Qf2; 7. Kf7!, Threatening 8. Qc8 and 9. Qg8 ‡.

7. ... Qh4; 8. Kf8,

Black resigned, because after 8. ... Qg5; follows 9. Qf7 and 10. Qg8 ‡.

An even better end game of the same kind took place during the German Championships in Dortmund 1973.

The Swedish Grandmaster, Ulf Andersson, joint winner of the German International Championships in Dortmund 1973, with Spassky and Hecht, although only

Andersson v. Kunstowicz

114

White wins

21 years of age, is already conversant with Queen endings in a masterful way!

1. ... Qb8;

Forced! Observe 1. ... Qd8;
2. Qh4 +, g5; 3. Qh6 +, Kf7;
4. Qe6 +, Kg7; 5. Q × g4, and Black cannot attack the Pawn on b5 with ... Qe8; because the Pawn on g5 would be captured by White's Queen, giving check at the same time.

2. Qd7!, Kg5; 3. Qg7, Qc8;

Or 3. ... Qe8; 4. Qh7!, Kf6;
5. Q × c7 wins

4. Kf1,

Kg2 straight away would have been better.

4. ... Qb8; 5. Ke2, Qc8; 6. Ke3, Qb8; 7. Ke2, Qc8; 8. Kf1, Qb8;
9. Kg1, Qc8; 10. Kg2, Qb8;

White had to watch carefully that *the same position would not occur three times over.* According to the rules—Article 12, Black could then have claimed a draw.

11. Qe7 +, Kh6;
  11. ... Kh5?; 12. Qh4 ⧣
12. Qh4 +, Kg7; 13. Q × g4, Qe8;
14. Qg5, Q × b5; 15. Qe7 +, Kh6;
16. Qd8!

Threatens checkmate in two moves with Qh8 +, Kg5; Qh4 ⧣

16. ... g5; 17. Q × c7, Qb4;

If Black had taken on d3, the Pawn on d6 would have been lost with check, and then the Pawn on e5 would also be captured.

18. Kh3, Kg6; 19. Qd7, Qc5;
20. Qf5 +, Kh6; 21. Kg4, Qc7;

As the Pawn on g5 will also be lost now, a decision cannot be far off. Soon the white King moves on to the Queen's wing to b5.

22. Q × g5 +, Kh7; 23. Qh5 +, Kg7; 24. Qe8, Kh7; 25. Qc6, Qd8;
26. Qb7 +, Kg8; 27. Kf3, Kh8;
28. Ke2, Kg8; 29. Kd2, Kf8;
30. Kc2, Kg8; 31. Kb3, Kf8;

See diagram 115.

The King executes the sentence

This impressive end game is coming to a close. It shows the strength of the (white) King in the ending. Meanwhile the black Queen has been degraded to the power of a Bishop.

32. Ka4, Kg8; 33. Kb5,
  And Black resigned.

115

116

Browne v. Planinc, Grandmaster
Tournament, Holland
1974

The stalemate trap

The American Grandmaster,
Walter Browne with White to
move, failed to concentrate for
just one moment:

1. f2 × e3??,

And victory was thrown away.
Firstly White should have given
the black King freedom of movement with 1. Qe8 +, Kh7;
2. Qd7 +, Kh8; then he could
have captured the Bishop on e3
in order to obtain a winning
margin with two more Pawns to
his credit. Now however he
succumbs to the well placed
stalemate trap:

1. ... Qh2 + !!

The sacrificial offer of the
Queen awakens White from his
dreams. His opponent achieves
a draw.

2. Kf3,

If 2. Kf1, Qf2 + !;

2. ... Qe2 + ;   3. Kg3,   Qg2 + ;
4. K × g2 a draw!

In spite of this mishap, Browne
finished the tournament as the
overall winner.

Solutions to the puzzles

No. 1 1. Qb3!, Ke7; 2. Q × e6 +,
K × e6; 3. Kc3, followed
by advancing the a Pawn,
etc.

No. 2 1. ... Bb5 + ; 2. Bc4, B ×
c4 + ; 3. b × c4, N × e2;
4. K × e2, Kc6 and wins in
similar fashion to the previous example.

No. 3 The white King gains the
opposition: 1. Kg2, Kb7;
2. Kf3, Ka6; 3. Ke3, Kb5;
4. Kd3, K × c5; 5. Kc3! a
draw.